The Packing Book

The Packing Book

SECRETS OF THE CARRY-ON TRAVELER

4th Edition

Judith Gilford

TEN SPEED PRESS
Berkeley | Toronto

In loving memory of my father, Morton Elkins

Ten Speed Press
P.O. Box 7123
Berkeley, CA 94707
www.tenspeed.com

Distributed in Australia by Simon and Schuster Australia, in Canada by Ten Speed Press Canada, in New Zealand by Southern Publishers Group, in South Africa by Real Books, and in the United Kingdom and Europe by Publishers Group UK.

Cover design by Chloe Rawlins
Text design by Tasha Hall
Text illustrations by Richard Sigberman

The Library of Congress has cataloged the earlier edition as follows:
Gilford, Judith.
    The packing book: secrets of the carry-on traveler / Judith Gilford.—Rev. ed.
        p. cm.
    Includes bibliographical references.
    ISBN 0-89815-821-4
    1. Travel I. Title
G151.G54 1996
910'.2'02-dc20   96-10864
    CIP

ISBN-13: 978-1-58008-783-4 (4th edition)
ISBN-10: 1-58008-783-3 (4th edition)

First printing this edition 2006
Printed in Canada

1 2 3 4 5 — 10 09 08 07 06

Contents

Acknowledgments

Many thanks to the following knowledgeable people and organizations for contributing interviews and materials: Overseas Adventure Travel (OAT); REI and REI Adventure Tours; Hostelling International/American Youth Hostels (AYH), for sharing the outstanding packing lists that are used in their adventure travel programs; wardrobe consultants Carol Bell, Joyce Beadle, Linda Curyea, Karen Snow, and Laura Santi; Keeble and Schuchat Photography; The Walk Shop; Tutto Luggage; Wilderness Institute; Sierra Designs; Ex Officio; Adventure Medical Kits; Travel Goods Association; International Luggage Repair Association (ILRA); Aris Export; Norm Thompson; Edwards Luggage; Bloomingdales Luggage; MEI; Flexo-Line; L.L.Bean; Remin Kart-a-Bag; Samsonite; Patagonia; Lullaby Lane; Nancy Gold, Tough Traveler; Travelpro; FAA Office of Public Affairs; Dee Donaldson; and Suzanne Hogsett.

Thanks also to all my family members and friends for their moral support, ideas, information, and babysitting; and especially to Kathleen Keough, Roger Rapoport, Peter Beren, Kai Wessels, George Young, Aaron Wehner, Heather Garnos, Nancy Austin, Rich Sigberman, Leili Eghbal, Cynthia Traina, Lisa Ryers, Lauren Webb, Victor Ichioka, Christa Laib, Frances Bowles, Sharilyn Hovind, Lisa Westmoreland, Annie Nelson, Julie Lavezzo, Michael Marcuson, Laura Sheppard, Sharon Todd, and the entire staff of Easy Going.

In memory of Larry Kruger, inventor of the "World Class Passport Carrier."

My continued love and gratitude to my husband, David, for his support and unwavering faith; to my teenage kids, Nathan and Sara, for their cheerful hugs, pride, and enthusiastic encouragement, as well as some fact-checking for this revision; to my mother, Thelma Elkins, founder of Easy Going, who has been telling me for years that "it oughtta be a book!" and to her husband, Dr. Mel Lipsett, who encouraged me to update a fourth edition.

Last but not least, in memory of my wonderful father, Mort Elkins, for his lifelong love, courage, optimism, and humor.

Preface

Dear Reader,

Since the first edition of *The Packing Book* was released in 1994, so much has changed! When I first started teaching the skill of packing light to the customers of Easy Going Travel Shop and Bookstore in Berkeley, California, my audience was a typical bunch of "independent" travelers. They wanted to go out on their own, off the beaten path, with little to hinder them in the way of material belongings. At that time "wheelaboard" luggage was a new invention, in its infancy. The idea of traveling "carry-on," was fairly new to most conventional travelers. *The Packing Book* was the first book to unveil the ins and outs of traveling light to the general public.

Today, in 2006, the travel landscape has completely changed. Traveling independently is no longer reserved for the backpack crowd traveling across Asia or Europe. Mobile travel has become mainstream; thus, many business and leisure travelers have taken up the notion that they too can travel light. They have discovered the benefits of paring down on the road: time savings, mobility, and simplicity.

The travel goods industry has recognized this trend. Luggage, travel clothing, and travel accessories markets have burgeoned with new products aimed at every type of traveler. Today's voyager can take advantage of high-tech materials and sophisticated designs that are compact, sturdy, practical, and cost effective.

As we all know, the travel environment has also transformed monumentally. Since the tragic events of September 11, 2001, security has become a major focus. What you can and can't bring with you is of concern now, and keeping up with regulations is important for every traveler. Luckily, the Internet makes this easy, since the government as well as all airlines have websites with explanations of their policies and rules.

In addition, the airlines are constantly looking at ways to cut down expenses, including decreasing flights, which makes large airplanes more crowded and the use of commuter-size planes more frequent. And it seems like *everyone* wants to go carry-on now! So arises a new problem—running out of space for carry-ons on the airplane!

For all these reasons, it is time to bring out an updated edition of *The Packing Book*. Pay special attention to such things as tips on security, what you can and cannot bring onboard, and what to do in case the overhead bins are full. Peruse recent products (which are always changing) and websites to brush up on problem-solving merchandise.

This book is meant to be fun. In every odyssey, preparation is part of the hero's journey. Visualize yourself on the road, traveling light. Make lists of what you want to bring, check them off twice, subtract half, and you will be ready to go! Give yourself time to ponder your options, and consider the difference between what you *think* you need to bring and what you *really* need in order to have a safe, pleasant, and serendipitous excursion.

To all of you, have an inspiring expedition!

—*Judy Gilford*

Introduction:
Singing the Overpacker's Blues

Welcome to Overpackers Anonymous! If you've ever experienced that sinking feeling while staring at your bed on the night before departure, clothes piled high and an open suitcase on the floor, this is the book for you. Perhaps you suffer from the "just-in-case" syndrome, convinced you have to take every piece of clothing you own on a two-week trip. Do you feel compelled to pack a different fashion garment for morning, noon, and night?

We all know the consequences—being weighed down by luggage, dependent on others for help, waiting in endless lines, and constantly managing "inventory." And for what? Most people don't use half of what they bring and swear that the next time will be different.

Don't worry—you're not alone. In my years of teaching packing seminars at Easy Going Travel Shop and Bookstore in Berkeley, California, and for large corporations, clothing stores, and civic organizations, I have discovered that everyone—even the most seasoned traveler—worries about packing. I do too! The overwhelming interest in *The Packing Book* has further proven that "packing anxiety" strikes a chord in every traveler, for good reason. You're leaving home for an unfamiliar destination, without the security of your familiar possessions. What if you underpack and leave home without some essential you need? What if you can't find what you need when you get there? "What if?" is the question that plagues us all.

Another problem is that every trip is different. You've just mastered packing for formal business trips, but then you decide to tack on a beach vacation, or the family decides to go for a weekend getaway. Sometimes you go by air, sometimes by car, or perhaps by train. Sometimes you don't care how much your bag weighs, while at other times traveling light is crucial in order to negotiate the trip. *The Packing Book* will be useful no matter what kind of trip you are taking *this time*. "This time" can mean a formal five-day business trip, a family weekend getaway, a week at a beach resort, or a three-week combination work and play vacation in two climates.

Finding balance is the key. Whether you go carry-on or decide to check your bag, you really can pack everything you need to feel comfortable on the road with a single manageable suitcase plus an optional secondary bag.

This book is designed to make you feel more confident about packing efficiently so that you can enjoy your full measure of mobility and independence on the road. I'll discuss what luggage to buy, what clothes to wear and how to maintain them on the road, what travel accessories you will need, and how to organize yourself in general. And I'll also show you a great packing technique.

With modern innovations in luggage, clothing fabrications, and portable travel gear, we travelers are fortunate to live in an age when traveling light has never been easier.

So have no fear, overpackers—you'll soon be on the road to recovery!

Your Traveling Lifestyle and a Flexible Packing Plan

Trips vary in the activities they entail, how mobile you want to be, and the level of choice that you want in your wardrobe and accessories. Some trips require more-formal clothing, whereas others are entirely casual. Sometimes you want to be self-sufficient and travel very light. At other times you want to have a bigger wardrobe and more accessories, even if the trade-off is heavier luggage. Sometimes you want as much variety as possible and will accept heavier luggage and perhaps even two pieces. But don't worry, because by using this book, you'll be able to get there "carry-on," whatever your traveling lifestyle! Those of you who plan to check your luggage will still learn to travel lighter by using this book.

Remember, planning is the essential key to anxiety-free packing. Even if you aren't leaving next week, read the background information so that when you're ready to hit the road, you will have put together a versatile wardrobe that you can pack in less time than you would have believed possible.

THE CARRY-ON
CRAZE

L et's play travel trivia. Here are three questions for you:

1. How many pieces of luggage are handled by the airlines each year?

2. How many pieces of luggage are lost by the airlines each year?

3. What happens to all that lost luggage?

Now, the answers. The airlines handle more than seven hundred million pieces of luggage annually. They lose approximately one percent. This isn't bad. But where does all that lost luggage end up? In Scottsboro, Alabama. The Unclaimed Baggage Center's fifty-thousand-square-foot retail store (and its companion website, www.unclaimedbaggage.com) has an inventory of over one million lost items. "We're seeing more laptops, cell phones, Palm Pilots, business suits, topcoats, cameras, anything that you have to take out and put through security checkpoints," says the Unclaimed Baggage Center's Joey Medlin. After the airlines have made every effort to find the owners and have failed to do so, the bags and their contents are sold, in wholesale lots. At the retail store, the merchandise is displayed in small storefronts and sold, retail, at discount prices.

And that's not all; there's more bad news. Travel has changed so much since the last edition of this book! Personal belongings in checked luggage have always been at risk of employee theft. But the enhanced security standards following the September 11, 2001, attacks have involved more people in the handling of luggage, and there is more perusal of your personal belongings as the X-ray machines ramp up to inspect them. Two agencies—the airline and the Transportation Security Administration (TSA)—now handle baggage. So many hands make for increased possibility of lost and pilfered luggage. And it is difficult to determine at what point in the process—screening, x-raying, handling—any pilfering might occur. What's more, nearly all airline carriers exclude valuables most likely to be stolen—electronics, camera equipment, jewelry, cash—from liability coverage. Checking luggage that contains valuables is not a wise idea.

Why Go Carry-on?

Fear of losing their luggage or belongings is not the only reason travelers want to carry their baggage on the plane. It's also faster: carrying your own luggage allows you to bypass the carousels at the airport and move right on to your destination. Business people are especially taken with carry-on, as they want to get off the plane and get right to their appointments (time is money). Some travelers prefer to be self-sufficient, especially when they are touring many destinations that are off the beaten track. Diverse modes of transportation while traveling often create the need to be able to manage luggage without help from porters, particularly when some airlines are now charging for curbside check-in.

And when you consider the rise of budget airlines like Southwest that do not offer interline baggage transfers, it makes sense to carry on. If you've checked baggage, your flight is late, and you are connecting to another airline, you may have a problem, particularly if your bag is slow coming off the luggage carousel at baggage claim. Also, some budget airlines make you pay to have your bag shipped to your final destination if it misses the flight. That's right:

if you check in less than half an hour before flight time your bag can be tagged as a "late check-in." If it misses the flight, for any reason, you, the passenger, are considered responsible for the bag not making the plane. You have a choice of waiting for the bag to show up on a later flight (which can be many hours or even a day later) or paying for overnight delivery of the bag to your final destination—not a pretty sight if you happen to be connecting to an international flight.

And let's not even get started on so-called point-to-point budget carriers like Europe's popular Ryan Air—they don't even guarantee they'll be able to transfer your checked luggage within their own network. If a flight is running late and your bag doesn't make a transfer between two Ryan Air planes, they are not responsible. Enough said.

Even if you are traveling by train, bus, or car, don't assume that you can bring lots of extra luggage. For one thing, trunk space in cars is limited. Moreover, for any one of a number of reasons you might find it necessary to add a flight to your journey. At this point you may be forced to ship your extra baggage at the post office, UPS, FedEx, or DHL because you didn't think you'd be flying this trip. Business and personal emergencies can force you to take an unexpected flight, and shedding luggage at the last minute can be difficult and time consuming.

When to Check

There are times, however, when carrying on luggage is neither necessary or practical—situations like these:

- You need to carry lots of equipment, beyond the carry-on limit.
- Your luggage is being handled for you by the tour company.
- You are traveling with small children and don't want to deal with luggage too.
- Your physical condition prevents you from handling your own luggage.

- You are traveling with a person with disabilities. Dealing with their equipment or a wheelchair may be all you can handle.

- You require bulky cold-weather clothing or gear.

- You are planning to shop and need lots of room for souvenirs.

- You are going on a formal business trip and need several suits or dresses.

- You are going on a trip that requires several suits, evening gowns, tuxedos, outfits, and so on.

- You are in the fashion business and must have ten pairs of shoes and sixteen outfits, all unrelated.

- In short, you have overpacked and must check a large suitcase!

Even if you plan to check your suitcase through, traveling with one carry-on bag makes it possible for you to go anywhere! The luggage will not be a burden at the hotel, in a taxi or train, or walking around.

For the rest of us, my carry-on strategy will simplify life on the road even further.

This book focuses on carry-on travel because more and more travelers are discovering that carry-on is not only desirable, but also feasible on all kinds of trips. The designs and fabrics of carry-on luggage have become very sophisticated. Leisure and business clothing is available in a variety of fabrics that are relatively wrinkle-resistant. Travel accessories and weather gear are available to provide comfort and protection without enormous bulk. And, as I'll show you, there is an effective technique for packing all of these items in a carry-on.

If you want to carry on your luggage, you will need to reorient your packing mentality. Carry-ons are a big change from the 29-inch suitcase you may be used to checking in. The reduced space means that you have to make choices about living on the road. Once you have chosen a traveling lifestyle, you will be able to choose a suitable wardrobe and accessories. This book will teach you to travel light.

Carry-on Guidelines

The determination to carry on all their luggage has driven passengers to board with anything and everything imaginable, from computers to giant toys to shopping bags full of pineapples. This might be convenient for the owners, but it wreaks havoc on the other passengers trying to board and on the safety standards promoted by the flight attendants. It is not uncommon for heavy items to rain down from overhead bins during turbulence, injuring passengers and crew. Airline unions have been agitating for stricter regulation and enforcement regarding the number of bags and sizes of carry-on luggage.

The Federal Aviation Administration states only that bags that are brought aboard must fit under the seat or in the overhead bin. Each airline is free to define its own limits on the number, size, and weight of carry-on luggage, and it is up to the gate attendants to be as lenient or as strict as they care to be.

Their decision is influenced by the size of the aircraft (commuter planes have less space than jumbo jets); whether the plane is full, half full, or empty; and whether it is a long international flight. Attendants may be more lenient toward passengers traveling in first and business class.

Size

Generally the upper limit for carry-on luggage to be stowed under the seat is 45 inches overall. When you add up the length, height, and depth of the bag (measured in inches), the sum should be no more than 45 inches. This includes suitcases measuring between 20 and 22 inches long—that is, 20 x 16 x 9 inches or 21 x 16 x 8 inches or 22 x 14 x 9 inches (the maximum size). The 8- or 9-inches-deep measurement is the crucial one here. Anything more than 10 inches deep will be hard to stuff overhead or under the seat. Keep in mind that softsided luggage will expand when packed, so don't overstuff it, or you'll have trouble stowing it. If I am traveling with a suitcase and a smaller tote bag, I like to distribute the weight between them so that I can easily lift my suitcase overhead. Sometimes this means packing heavier items (such as gear and toiletries) in my day bag that I can stow underneath my seat.

Carry-on sizes vary according to the type of airplane you are flying in. Some airlines will allow only 39 total inches under the seat, room enough for a small tote bag (about 17 inches long). Foreign-based airlines (which also tend to be more strict), international flights, commuter airlines, and airlines using smaller aircraft are more likely to have lower limits. Keep in mind that different aircraft used by the same airline will have different-sized compartments. It is best to call ahead to *each airline you plan to fly* and ask about its carry-on regulations. Get the information sent or faxed to you so that you can carry it with you to avoid arbitrary decisions by airline staff. On some aircraft, aisle seats tend to have a bit less luggage space, so if you have a full-sized underseat bag, ask for a window or middle seat.

The upper limit for the overhead compartment on many airlines is 60 inches overall. This will accommodate larger, wider items such as folded garment bags, which may measure 22 x 8 x 23 inches. However, on many aircraft, the compartment is much smaller. To be on the safe side, *keep the length of your suitcase or garment bag (folded in half) to about 22 inches.* Longer items will be dealt with on a case-by-case basis. For safety's sake, try to keep the overhead compartment for larger, more-stable suitcases or light smaller ones. Luggage carts should be collapsed and placed under your seat.

How Many?

Most airlines allow you one or two pieces of carry-on luggage. You are also allowed to check through one or two other items, for a total of three or four pieces of luggage. So if you are planning to check additional luggage through, be sure to find out from each airline you plan to fly on what your *total* luggage allotment is, with any weight limitations, and how much of it may be carried on.

Counted as carry-on pieces are garment bags, suitcases, briefcases, travelpacks, daypacks, tote bags, camera cases, computers and computer cases, shopping bags, and duty-free bags.

NOTE: You are allowed *up to* a total circumference of 45 inches for underseat luggage, so two small bags that will fit underneath together count as one.

TIP: Some airlines and smaller aircraft may allow only one carry-on. Be sure to check with your airline!

About Garment Bags and Carriers

These "hanging closets" let you pack your clothes on hangers. A garment bag holds two to four garments. A garment carrier can hold ten or more garments on hangers. (I'll refer to both as garment bags.) Garment bags have their place as carry-on luggage. The general size limitation is 72 inches, or 45 x 4 x 23 inches (open). Some bags fold in half; others are tri-fold models. Garment bags are useful if you are on a business trip or vacation for which you'll need multiple suits or formal dresses. If not stuffed too full, they can be brought aboard and stowed in a closet or, folded in half, in the overhead bin. Many people like being able to hang everything up all at once at the hotel.

However, garment bags have limitations. First, most aircraft have little or no closet space in which to stow these heavy "mobile homes." If you don't get there first, the closet will be full and you will have to stow the bag overhead or check it. Second, meeting the closet's 8-inch-deep limitation will be impossible if the garment bag is packed with the usual requirements for a two- or three-week trip. Folded over, the bag may be too fat to fit overhead, so you will have to check it. Garment bags are also unwieldy to lug if you are taking public transportation on your own, although some models, such as Samsonite's Silhouette 5, feature wheels and a retractable handle.

For those reasons, garment bags are not my first choice. Much more useful is a 21- or 22-inch carry-on suitcase in the form of a shoulder bag, convertible pack, or wheeled bag, with a "suiter" option to accommodate a suit or jacket.

TIP: Choose a 22-inch suitcase as a carry-on. Anything longer must be checked!

Additional Carry-on Items

As well as one or two carry-on bags, most airlines allow you to take on board with you other miscellaneous items. These generally, but not always, include a handbag, overcoat or wrap, umbrella, binoculars, camera (35mm or digital without carrying case), a reasonable quantity of reading material, prosthetic devices (canes, braces, crutches), and unopened liquor, which, if you want to drink, must be served to you by the flight attendant. Travelers with infants are usually allowed an infant-necessities bag, a blanket, a small stroller that can fit overhead, and/or possibly a car seat, if there is room on the plane. Luggage carts may or may not be counted.

Security: Permitted and Prohibited Items

Since September 11, the travel environment has changed as security has been an increasing concern for all forms of transport. Pay close attention to what is permitted and prohibited in both carry-on luggage and checked luggage. The Transportation Security Administration (TSA) regulates transport of personal toiletries, medicine and medical supplies, and other personal belongings as well as hazardous materials. The following guidelines reflect recent changes by TSA. For a more complete listing visit www.tsa.gov/public.

Permitted Items in Carry-on Luggage

Personal items: Corkscrews, cuticle cutters, eyeglass-repair tools, eyelash curlers, crochet and knitting needles (circular are best), plastic or round-bladed butter knives, nail clippers, nail files, personal care toiletries with aerosols in limited quantities (such as hairsprays, deodorant), safety and disposable razors, blunt scissors with blades under 4 inches, toy transformer robots, toy weapons (not realistic), tweezers, umbrellas and walking sticks (both require inspection first).

Medication and special needs devices: Braille note-taker, slate and stylus, augmentation devices; diabetes-related supplies and equipment (must be inspected first); nitroglycerine pills or spray for medical use (if properly marked with professionally printed label); ostomy scissors (blades under 4 inches); prosthetic device tools and appliances.

Electronic devices: Camcorders, camera equipment,* laptop computers, mobile phones, pagers, PDAs.

Permitted in checked luggage only: Knives and scissors of any length; all sporting bats, sticks, clubs, cues, poles, and spears; ammunition; compressed-air guns, stun guns, and shocking devices; martial-arts and self-defense items.

Prohibited Items

The following hazardous items, among others, are prohibited in carry-on or checked luggage: flammables, mace, tear gas and other eye irritants, propane, butane cylinders or refills, cigarette lighter refills, any equipment containing fuel, safety or "strike anywhere"

---

* *The checked-luggage screening equipment will damage undeveloped film in camera equipment. TSA recommends putting undeveloped film (and cameras with undeveloped film in them) in your carry-on luggage and asking security at checkpoint to conduct an inspection by hand.*

matches, solvents, and aerosols. Call your airline or visit www. faa.gov regarding any specific hazardous items you are concerned about.

Using Portable Electronic Devices on the Plane
As this book goes to press, federal regulations prohibit airline passengers from using cell telephones or two-way radios on board. Many other devices can be taken on board, but their use is prohibited while the plane is taxiing, taking off, and landing. Each airline has the right to impose its own regulations, and flight crews can impose stricter ones if necessary. Here are some examples. Call your airline to verify pertinent information.

Items generally allowed to operate during flight: Portable voice recorders, electric shavers, calculators, laptop computers with attached mice, accessory printers and tape drives, handheld electronic games without remote controls, CD players, electronic toys without remote controls, video camcorders (sometimes not allowed), video players, tape cassette players, beepers, audio tape players, and pagers.

Items generally not allowed: Radios, AM and FM transmitters and receivers, televisions, mobile phones, electronic games, toys and computers with remote controls, cordless computer mice, and CB radios and other transmitting devices.

More Isn't Better–The *Real* Carry-on Allotment

Having just read the list of all the things that airlines allow you, right now you overpackers are probably thinking, "Great! I can take *everything* with me."

A gentle reminder: Carry-on is not about lugging all your worldly possessions with you wherever you go. Carry-on is about mobility, about freedom, about traveling *light.* The focus of this book is on planning, selecting, and taking *only what you need.*

If you prefer to check your luggage, limit yourself to a 24 inch bag. You can still use the information here to travel lighter.

NOTE: Our definition of *carry-on* will be *one* manageable carry-on bag that will fit underneath the seat or in the overhead bin on the airplane and in storage facilities when you are traveling around. For added convenience or a measure of luxury, you may also want to bring a second smaller bag such as a tote or daypack.

Carry-on Courtesy and Boarding Tips

Don't let carry-on travelers get a bad rap from their fellow passengers, who routinely complain about their transgressions. Follow these tips—especially if flights are over 60 percent full.

1. Arrive early for your flight, at least an hour before departure time, ninety minutes if it's a busy time, and two hours for overseas flights. If you have any metal implants such as a knee or hip replacement, want to request privacy during your potential TSA pat-down search, or are concerned about going through additional screening, I strongly recommend that you be in the security line at least ninety minutes before your flight. If you're running late for your flight and you have to go through additional screening, it's much easier to inadvertently leave valuables behind at check-in. Also try to avoid carrying metal items in your pockets. It's quicker to have your change, cell phone, and other metal items in a single bag. Keep in mind that some airports, like Frankfurt, require passengers to go through security screening twice. You will also have to pass through security screening after you clear customs and head for a domestic flight.

2. Board the flight as early as you can. This is critical. You will have more time to find your seat and a space for your luggage without bumping into other passengers.

3. Take only the number and size of bags allowed by each airline you plan to fly—usually just one carry-on and a purse, laptop, or other small bag.

4. Each overhead bin is for the belongings of two to three people. Do not take more than your own space. Don't use your space and then go hunting five or ten rows back for additional storage.

5. When boarding and disembarking, handle your bags carefully so you don't bump people in front of or behind you. Be patient.

6. The bulk of in-flight injuries are caused by luggage tumbling down from the overhead bins at the end of a flight. To avoid injuring passengers and crew:

   a. Tuck away or remove garment bag hooks. These catch on other bags and cause everything to tumble down.

   b. Choose fabric over smooth leather business cases, which can easily slide out and fall on other passengers.

7. Pack lightly enough that you can lift your main bag into the overhead compartment yourself, without having to rely on an attendant to help you. Place heavier items in your smaller bag and store it under your seat. Luggage carts go under the seat as well.

8. If you have a rigid-frame bag, such as a wheelaboard, plan on putting it overhead unless it is 20 inches long. It is very hard to maneuver rigid bags into the underseat compartment.

9. Aisle seats tend to have a bit less luggage space, so if you have a full-size underseat bag, ask for a window or middle seat. Emergency exit rows have better legroom and easier access to underseat spaces, too.

Gate-Checked Luggage

Gate checking occurs when your arrive at the gate or board the plane, and the crew deems it necessary to store your bag in the cargo hold instead of in the overhead bins. This usually occurs when a flight is full (another reason to board the plane early to ensure sufficient space in the overhead bins) or when the aircraft is small and does not have the same amount of space available for carry-ons as a larger plane You will have to check your carry-on at the gate and then pick it up at the arrival gate (not at baggage claim) when you arrive. Be sure to ask the flight attendant where you should pick up your gate-checked bag. The gate-checked bags on small planes are usually put on a cart, and after you deplane at your destination, you will pick up the bag from another cart at the bottom of the ramp or at the end of the jetway. However, if you are required to gate check your bag on a larger plane, this bag will show up at baggage claim with other checked luggage.

Gate Checking: Security Issues

Do not leave laptops, computer media, cameras, cell phones, planners, passports, or valuables in a gate-checked bag for a commuter flight. Carry them on in your small bag. You can, if necessary, even carry that camera around your neck. If all the overhead bins are full and you have to check your prescription medicine, valuable work papers, or an important present, you can claim for monetary damages, but that doesn't mean you will be able to retrieve any of these irreplaceable items. Unlike baggage claim, where you can stand and watch your bags arrive on the carousel, gate-checked bags waiting on the rack can easily be mistaken for someone else's or stolen while you are still disembarking from the plane.

To Be Prepared for Gate Checking

Always graciously check your luggage if the attendant deems it necessary. Label your luggage inside and out, lock your bags, and keep your hotel itinerary in an outside pocket in case your luggage arrives after you do.

If you have packed valuables in your suitcase that must be gate checked, you can use this strategy. Before giving up your bag, wait a bit, take your suitcase aside, open it and take out your "last-minute" or fold-up nylon bag. Then retrieve your valuables, transfer them to your fold-up bag, and check your suitcase. Put the nylon bag under your seat.

TIP: Use your nylon fold-up bag to transfer contents from an overstuffed carry-on so that it will fit in the overhead bin. You can empty the outside expandable pocket found on many bags or even take your bundle out! (See chapter 6.)

2

SMART LUGGAGE

Choosing the right luggage is crucial to traveling light. The wrong bag can defeat you if it is too heavy, uncomfortable to carry, cheaply made, the wrong size or style, or not weatherproof. The right piece of luggage can help you be an organized, self-sufficient traveler, will be a dream to pack, and will be easy to manage.

There are three types of luggage suitable for carry-on travel: the 45-inch carry-on suitcase or travelpack (21 or 22 inches in length), the hanging garment bag, and the tote bag or daypack. If you are determined to go carry-on and travel freely, limit yourself to the 45-inch bag as your main bag. Properly packed, it can handle almost any kind of wardrobe. If mobility is not essential or you have a larger, bulkier wardrobe, consider the garment bag. You can make use of plastic dry-cleaning bags (see p. 241) and the garment bag provides a convenient hanging closet when you reach your destination. If you intend to check your luggage or simply want more room, a 24-inch suitcase is your best bet.

Garment carriers are great for extended business trips as well as for cruises that require a lot of formal wear, but they do have their limitations. They are not reliable carry-ons. Airplane closets fill up quickly. As a result, you may have to fold your bag into an overhead compartment. If the bag is packed lightly, it will fit overhead, but if it's packed fully and folded in half, it could be too thick for the overhead compartment and will then have to be gate checked.

Garment bags are also unwieldy to carry about while sightseeing and may be difficult to stow in lockers or on public transportation.

Coordinating a Luggage System

When buying luggage, don't think of only individual pieces. Think of selecting a system—a configuration that enables you to be as mobile and hands-free as possible. You will be traveling with a main bag and a smaller secondary bag. When choosing your pieces, think of how they all will work together for comfort when boarding and disembarking, walking long distances, and loading and unloading. Look for ergonomic designs that decrease pressure on your hands and shoulders. Don't overload your shoulders. Always try to have one hand free to open doors, make phone calls, or write a note.

Your Main Bag: Choosing a 45-inch Carry-on

Your largest bag will hold the bulk of your clothing and some or all of your gear. Useful 45-inch carry-on styles (21 or 22 inches in length) include the shoulder bag, the travel pack (convertible backpack), and the wheeled bag. *To be able to pack as described in this book (see chapter 6), choose a bag with a zipper that goes around three side of the bag so that it can be opened like a book.*

In choosing a bag, consider the following:

- How the bag opens
- How heavy the bag is
- How you want to carry it (on your shoulders, on your back, by its own wheels, or a combination of these)
- How much you will be carrying it (take into account walking distances, types of transportation, and activities)
- Terrain and handling conditions (Will you encounter stairs, cobblestone streets, hiking trails? Will you be mostly indoors

or outdoors? Will there be dust and mud? How will it be transported?)

- How you want to organize and pack it
- Your long-term traveling needs

Shoulder Bags

The shoulder bag is a suitcase with a handle and a detachable shoulder strap. Semisoft versions have a structured frame created by piping and foam padding that maintains the bag's shape during packing. Their main attraction is ease of organization: they come in one-, two-, and three-compartment designs. They also compress easily to fit into tight spaces. My favorite brand is the Easy Going Special Edition Bag (see below). Other quality models are made by Boyt, Andiamo, Lands' End, L.L.Bean, REI, Patagonia, Caribou, Eagle Creek, and Tough Traveler. If you are carrying a fully loaded shoulder bag, I recommend taking a luggage cart as well.

A three-compartment, 45-inch carry-on shoulder bag.

Three-Compartment Shoulder Bags

A three-compartment bag, such as the 21-inch Easy Going Special Edition, is the perfect high-capacity, all-purpose bag for short trips (2–5 days), extended casual trips (6 days and up), or trips requiring two distinct wardrobes. Make sure that at least two of the compartments where you will pack clothing can be opened completely. You can stow warm-weather casual clothing in one section, business or cold-weather wear in the second, and use the third compartment for your gear. These bags are packing-friendly because each compartment is supported by piping and foam padding and keeps its shape during packing. Wardrobes fit snugly, so they wrinkle less. The Easy Going bag has easy-to-grasp, lockable zipper pulls, a comfortable handle and shoulder straps, and a top-loading outer compartment that prevents small accessory items from falling out. A new design features a horizontal strap across the back that allows it to be secured on top of another rolling bag. I use an Easy Going Special Edition Bag for business or leisure, for weekend, weeklong, and longer trips. For weekends I have shared it with my husband and kids!

TIP: If you will be carrying a shoulder bag for more than a short distance, I recommend using a luggage cart; like all shoulder bags, it can feel heavy quickly.

Two-Compartment Shoulder Bags
Two-section bags are useful for short trips (2–5 days) and simple wardrobes. They allow the traveler to separate clothing from accessories or the washed from the unwashed. Additional outside pockets help organize accessories.

One-Compartment Shoulder Bags
People like one-compartment suitcases because they are so easy to pack and a single zipper provides access to all their belongings. Wheels, a selling point for many travelers, are available only on one-compartment bags. Some, such as Tutto's carry-on suitcase, come with four wheels and a pullbar. Others, like the Travelpro Crew5 and most other wheelaboards, come with two built-in wheels and a telescoping handle.

A one-compartment suitcase, packed with the bottom layer of accessories.

Travel Packs (Convertible Backpacks)

The travel pack, sometimes called a convertible backpack, has become popular because it is versatile and easily carried. Designed by backpacking companies, it is incredibly sturdy, and many models can stand up to rough travel and handling conditions. This suitcase can transform itself. When carried horizontally, it is a

A travel pack (convertible backpack) with detachable daypack.

single-cavity shoulder bag. When turned vertically, it can be converted to a backpack: a hip belt and shoulder straps are stowed in the back panel. If you are doing a lot of sightseeing or walking or need to run for connections, it is a real blessing to be able to transfer 80 percent of the weight of your luggage off of your shoulders and onto your hips. Many travel packs come with extra features such as side pockets and a detachable daypack (which can act as your second piece of luggage). Keep in mind that, to meet carry-on regulations, such accessories must be emptied or detached for the flight.

Travelers planning to carry on their luggage must choose a convertible pack according to size (the main compartment must be no more than 9 x 14 x 22 inches). Many travel packs come in larger sizes. Unfortunately, they are too large to carry on. Manufacturers of good-quality carry-on travel packs include MEI, Eagle Creek, Rick Steves, Victorinox, REI, Patagonia, L.L.Bean, JanSport, Caribou, and Tough Traveler.

There are two types of travel packs suitable for general travel: frameless and internal frame.

Frameless Travel Packs

"Convenience level" travel packs come with padded shoulder straps and a padded waistband but have no other substantial means of support, such as an internal frame. You can carry this model on your back or sling one strap over your shoulder for that last dash at the airport. These packs are suitable for light packers and kids, when loads do not exceed 20 pounds. They are lighter and less expensive than packs with an internal frame.

Examples of frameless packs are the MEI Convertible suitcase and the Rick Steves Travelpack.

Internal-Frame Travel Packs

The "intermediate level" internal-frame travel packs make it easy to carry heavier loads. Designed to adjust to your torso length, these bags are mounted on hidden aluminum stays that give the pack stability. A foam or plastic sheet offers back support and cushioning protection from poking items. Typically these packs feature adjustable shoulder, hip, and sternum straps and a lumbar pad. Extras may include a zip-off day pack and expandable outside pockets. The pack may also have lash straps so that you can attach a sleeping bag or other gear. Some travel packs feature a telescoping handle and wheels, so they act like a wheelaboard as well (see below). Many companies make these bags; examples of internal frame travel packs are the MEI Voyageur, Flying Scotsman I, and Trekker I; Eagle Creek Journey; and Tough Traveler Super Padre.

"Advanced level" internal-frame packs offer features that you would look for on more technical packs, such as beefier waistbands, shoulder straps, and the like. Indeed, these packs can be used for backpacking as well as general travel, which may fit your long-term plans. Victorinox makes the excellent Nth 3200 Advanced Conversion Pack.

Internal-frame packs have three advantages: they are versatile, easily carried, and comfortable. If you want to buy only one bag for year-round use as conventional luggage and for outdoor activities such as hiking or backpacking, buy this style. It will give you the maximum freedom for sightseeing, hiking, and touring around with your luggage in tow. The attached daypack on many models makes it a self-contained unit when you are traveling. Internal-frame packs can be fitted to your body, providing the most comfort for a wide range of activities.

All packs differ in fit. Buy the one that fits you the best and still meets carry-on regulations. If your torso is long and fit is important for the activities you plan, you may have to choose a larger size and forgo the convenience of carrying it on the aircraft.

Travel Packs with Wheelaboard Option

These hybrid bags are extremely popular because they offer the option of being carried on your back like a regular pack or of being pulled along like a wheeled suitcase. The Eagle Creek Switchback Series and Victorinox Trek Pack Plus are excellent examples. These bags feature ergonomic designs that offer the comfort of shoulder and lumbar support but also a telescoping handle and in-line wheels that allow you to transform the bag into a durable wheeled unit. For a trip that combines the rugged with the cosmopolitan, this may be the bag for you. However, these bags can be quite heavy on their own, so make sure you can lift it when full.

Wheeled Suitcases

TIP: Your suitcase should open up like a book. You should also choose a bag that is fairly unobstructed inside. Too many bells and whistles—such as pockets and pouches or a frame that reduces the internal space—can limit the room you have to pack your clothing. Finally, watch the weight. Can you lift it overhead or up the stairs?

Wheeling one's luggage seems to be irresistible. But before you select wheeled luggage or a luggage cart, assess your needs. If you need one carry-on, a wheeled suitcase or a lightweight luggage cart may be the answer to your prayers. But if you will be walking on rough terrain, doing some hiking, or climbing lots of stairs, think twice about taking a conventional wheelaboard—instead, look into the hybrid models (such as the convertible packs) just

Tutto's 24-inch pull-along.

discussed. If you are a constant traveler who carries large loads, or if you tend to load the cart with extras, you may need a heavy-duty luggage cart with regular luggage. Extra weight on wheeled suitcases or lightweight carts can cause the handle to bend or even break. Keep in mind that the more hardware there is, the more there is to break!

Wheelaboards feature a rigid frame, telescoping handle, and built-in wheels. I favor the simpler, nonexpandable models that won't let you overpack. However, many of them are expandable for use on the ground. On all models, it is possible to attach a second tote, briefcase, or even a folded garment bag on top of the built-in bag so that you can travel unencumbered.

There are wheeled models designed to appeal to every traveler's needs. Wheelaboards come in all shapes and sizes, from 20-inch underseaters to large 29-inch suitcases. For our purposes, stick to the 22-inch carry-on size. If you insist on more room, the 24-inch will still allow mobility on the ground but must be checked through.

Most wheeled models are vertically oriented, with two wheels. However, Healthy Luggage by Tutto features four sturdy wheels riveted to a nearly indestructible external frame. The bag's weight rests on the ground, not against your body. A U-shaped pull bar is anchored to the outer edges of the frame. This provides extra stability for fingertip control and easy 360-degree maneuverability. The Tutto bag can be loaded on top with other bags or even sat upon! People with arthritis or back problems will find these models particularly helpful. For this reason, Tutto was the winner of the Arthritis Foundation Design Award.

All wheeled models are one-compartment suitcases and come in several styles.

Standard models have a spacious inner compartment, with amenities such as inside pockets along the side and tie-down straps. Suiter models allow you to hang a jacket, suit, or dress and fold it inside the top lid. This is an important innovation and a real boon for business and leisure travelers.

Wheelaboards are perfect for concourses, airports, and conventional urban travel. When shopping, check for a strong frame, ergonomic handle, good finish work, coil zippers that go around three sides of the bag so that it opens like a book, and sturdy rubber or urethane rollers, or in-line–skate wheels that are inset in the bag. Travelpro adds a "No-Tip Foot" so that the expanded bag does not fall forward when it is stood up.

Wheelaboard with suiter option.

For maximum packability, select thin walls and as much unobstructed inner space as possible. You want the full $19^{1}/_{2}$ to $21^{1}/_{2}$ inches for packing! Watch that the telescoping handle casing does not take up too much room on the inside of the case. For this reason, I favor models such as Travelpro Travelite and Victorinox, which have plenty of unobstructed space inside.

The telescoping handles should be easy to open and close (do you need to use one hand or two?) and should lock in the open and closed positions. There are many types of handles, and they are not interchangeable—make sure you can quickly and easily acquire replacement parts for servicing if needed. Some models feature an "ergonomic" handle that takes the pressure off of your hands and arms as you pull the bag. Two grab handles, one at the top and one at the side, are handy for easy lifting.

Pick the configuration of outside pockets that suits you. Gusseted pockets are more easily accessed and hold more than flat slash pockets. If more room is what you want, look for outside pockets that expand. Just keep in mind that when the bag is fully expanded it will no longer fit in the overhead bins! It may also be too heavy for you to lift as needed. Avoid this trap by carrying a nonexpandable suitcase and a second tote or daypack.

Collapsibility can be handy. Tutto luggage collapses to $3^1/2$ inches flat for under-the-bed storage—no more waiting in long lines to retrieve your luggage at the end of a cruise!

There are many, many brands of wheelaboards in all price ranges. Andiamo, Atlantic, Briggs and Reilly, Boyt, Eagle Creek, Hartmann, Kiva, Lark, Samsonite, Travelpro, Tumi, Tutto Healthy Luggage, and Victorinox are all quality brands.

Vertical wheelaboard with telescopic handle.

Choosing a Garment Bag

A garment bag can act as your main bag. There are numerous garment bags on the market, in all price ranges. As with all luggage, choose the one that fits your needs. Consider first the length of your trips as well as the clothing you will need. Garment bags are suitable for suits, dresses, evening gowns, tuxedos, and hanging dress shirts. Hanging bags come in two- to four-suit depths, and may be 42, 48, 52, or 56 inches long. If you choose a longer version, look for a bag that will fold into thirds so as to fit under the seat or overhead. A simple garment cover will protect that one tuxedo or wear-it-once formal outfit or suffice for an overnight trip. Some bags come with wheels.

A semisoft garment bag is piped to keep its structure. Make sure the outside hook is detachable or stowable so it does not dangle. A bar at the top supports the weight the bag is designed for. Do not overpack, or the bar may bend. Access to the hangers is important, too. Convenient models have a self-supported swing-out curtain. The curtain opens like a door, allowing full access to the interior. A handy hook keeps the curtain out of the way as you pack.

Look for a lightweight, weather- and stain-resistant fabric, such as Cordura or ballistic nylon. The hanger system (such as the Wally Lock) should allow use of regular wire hangers and prevent clothes from falling off. Make sure the handle is comfortable. Zipper openings should be oriented correctly regardless of whether the bag is in the folded or extended position. Many bags have pockets for accessories, shoes, and soiled clothing; look for an organizational setup you like. Tie straps inside are handy.

NOTE: Make sure that the top outside hanger clip can be removed or stowed easily. These dangling hardware pieces often get caught on other items in the overhead bin during flight and are a major cause of passenger injuries when they cause other items to tumble down at the end of a flight.

Your Second Bag: Choosing a Tote Bag or Daypack

It is convenient to have access to items you need on the plane and during the day without having to return to your main bag. Daypacks, shoulder totes, and duffels can hold a small wallet with the day's money, a sweater, a quick change of clothes, medicine, glasses, water bottle, guidebook, map, writing materials, tissues, lip balm, sunscreen, makeup, a small camera, and so on. Business travelers will want something for a cell phone, computer, and computer equipment, files and business materials, as well as personal items. (See also Camera, Computer, and Business Bags on p. 28.) People who may be walking a lot or doing day hikes will definitely prefer the daypack.

For the plane, in case your main bag is checked, consider stocking your hand luggage with an extra shirt, set of underwear, and toiletries, so that you will not be entirely inconvenienced if the bag is lost. *Your second bag should be lockable.*

The "Last-Minute" Bag

In addition to or instead of your second bag, there is one more item that I consider an absolute must for every traveler: a sturdy fold-up zippered nylon bag that expands to become a suitcase or daypack. Stowed away in your suitcase and taking up almost no space, it can be taken out at a moment's notice. It can act as a shopping bag, a laundry bag, or a day bag to carry your belongings if you will be out all day. You can use it to bring home souvenirs and extras. The last-minute bag can also be extremely useful on the airplane. For example, if the attendant requests that you gate check your bag, you can quickly step aside, take out your last-minute bag from your suitcase, retrieve your valuables, and transfer them to the nylon bag, which can be stowed comfortably beneath your seat (see p. 14).

Daypacks

The daypack is the most versatile and comfortable second bag for the casual traveler. A daypack can be worn on the back or shoulders, leaving your hands free. You can use it on day hikes, stowing your suitcase in a locker or hotel room. Choose a daypack made of lightweight parachute nylon, pack-cloth, or Cordura nylon. Many travel packs conveniently come with a detachable daypack as part of the unit, which is invaluable when boarding and disembarking.

Or pack a lightweight collapsible model in your suitcase for use when needed on the road.

Select a model with at least one pocket on the outside, padded shoulder straps, and a handle at the top. Double zippers allow easy access when the bag is stowed. Attach a combination lock and you have a fairly safe place for your camera.

Tote Bags

Lightweight totes are good for general touring. If you will be out all day and into the evening without returning to your hotel, you will want a tote big enough to hold a quick change of clothing, shoes, or accessories, plus your umbrella, raincoat, guidebook, and camera. There are a variety of styles by all major manufacturers. All bags should lock. Choose one that coordinates in function with your main bag. (For example, many wheelaboards coordinate with a tote bag that attaches to the telescoping handle.) The last-minute bag (see p. 27) can also act as a tote. Ameribag make the ergonomic Healthy Back Bag, which makes the weight feel lighter by redistributing the bag's center of gravity while relieving stress on the neck, shoulders, and back. It can be worn on the shoulder or across the back.

Waistpacks

Some people like a waistpack instead of a tote bag for traveling. I find that these are not versatile (they cannot hold a sweater, umbrella, or extra shoes) plus they are bulky to pack. Also, they target you as a "tourist" immediately. If you do travel with one, for extra security be sure to thread the waistband through your belt loops. *Do not use a waistpack for valuables such as passport, money, tickets, credit cards, and so on. Those should be carried only in a security wallet.* (See chapters 3 and 11.)

Camera, Computer, and Business Bags

Camera bags, briefcases, and laptop computer bags are considered to be carry-on luggage. Therefore, you need a multifunctional bag that will hold your camera or computer equipment as well as other business and personal items. These bags come in every configuration imaginable, made by almost all of the major luggage, photography, and outdoor companies. Pick a case that is high quality, comfortable to wear, and easy to work from. For security reasons, I prefer inconspicuous styles and a locking case.

NOTE: Smooth-sided briefcases are a major cause of in-flight injuries. They fall out when the overhead bins are opened. For safety reasons, consider a fabric bag instead of leather.

Aside from standard briefcases, travelers can choose a casual-looking but sturdy, padded briefcase shoulder bag with adjustable inserts for computer equipment. Look for these in outdoor, photography, luggage, and travel stores. I like models that have a place for a water bottle on the outside. Also, some wheelaboard lines, such as Travelpro, offer computer and camera cases that attach to your wheelaboard. Tutto makes a very fine "Office-on-Wheels," a 20 x 13 x 8-inch case with an external frame and four wheels that is pulled by a U-shaped pullbar. I like it because it is top loading for easy access and can carry a heavy load easily (so you don't have to). It's particularly good when you have samples, binders, catalogs, paper, computer equipment, and the like, and excellent for people with back problems or arthritis.

Active photographers and adventure travelers should take two bags. One larger bag holds all of your equipment and can be combined with a computer. Lowepro make the excellent Trekker series. The CompuTrekker AW can hold digital camera equipment plus a laptop. It can be worn as a daypack.

There are also hybrid rolling/daypack bags, such as Lowepro's Rolling Mini Trekker AW or Tamrac's Big Wheels Rolling Photo Backpack.

An additional smaller camera case will enable you to lighten up for a hike or a ramble around town. All of the camera bag manufacturers make great models. You may prefer a waistpack or modular bag because they allow maximum mobility and leave the hands free. Movable dividers enable configuration of the bag to make room for everything from a long lens to a video recorder.

Lowepro's Orion Trekker, a waistpack-style camera bag, includes a separate snap-on daypack for clothing, food, and necessities. When not needed, the daypack folds neatly into the front pocket of the bag.

Quality camera bags are made by Tenba, Tamrac, Lowepro, Domke, Sun Dog, Ruff-Pack, and Billingham. (For tips on carrying film, see p. 71.)

NOTE: Video tapes, computer disks, and credit cards can all be ruined by the magnetic field found in the metal detector at the airport. **Put these items through the X-ray and not the metal detector.** Although X-rays can also damage high-speed film, the effects are cumulative, so once is probably fine. If you are uncertain, you can ask for a visual inspection of your camera. One way to avoid this problem is to develop your film en route, before you get on the plane. Digital memory cards are not affected by the metal detector or X-ray machines.

Look for these features when shopping for camera and computer bags:

- The outer shell materials should provide protection against impact, abrasion, tearing, and the weather. Ballistic nylon or Cordura nylon should be 1,000-denier or more, with a weather-resistant urethane coating. The two fabrics are equally strong, but ballistic nylon is less abrasion resistant and looks more elegant than Cordura does. Cordura is more abrasion and slash resistant. Canvas is not as waterproof or as rugged as synthetics are, but it is lighter, less expensive, more abrasion resistant, and conforms more readily to body shape.

- Make sure that the inner padding is made of closed-cell foam or other lightweight composite padding, not open-cell foam, which will flatten or degrade over time.

- Look for versatile padded insert walls with movable partitions.

- Make sure that the buckles, rings, and zippers are of high quality, easy to use, and resistant to cold weather.

- Make sure the pockets have storm flaps for protection in wet weather.

- Look for a rigid floor, which prevents the sides from caving in when the bag is lifted.

For more information on travel photography, read *PCPhoto Magazine*, "Essential Travel Gear," June 2004.

General Luggage-Buying Guidelines

When buying new luggage, the old adage "you get what you pay for" really is true. There are all types of luggage in all price categories, and they may look surprisingly similar. But performance is almost always related to price. Luggage differs in its ability to withstand the demands of travel and modern-day baggage-handling systems. Its performance depends upon the quality of the fabric, frame, zipper, handle, and hardware that is used and on its general workmanship. Keep in mind that what seems expensive in the short run will save you money and inconvenience in the long run.

Define what it is that you expect from your luggage and buy accordingly. The Travel Goods Association recommends that you purchase luggage to meet your most demanding traveling needs. People who travel extensively for business or for adventure, or who often check through their luggage, have different luggage needs than those who enjoy occasional leisurely travel. Your luggage retailer can help you make the best purchase if you tell the staff your needs and expectations.

Read the luggage warranty carefully. Know what types of damage the manufacturer does and does not cover. Normal, cosmetic wear and tear will generally not be covered, but a manufacturer's defects, such as a handle that breaks, a wheel that comes off, or a zipper that fails, will generally be repaired or replaced by the manufacturer or retailer. Try to choose a retailer and manufacturer that will service your luggage quickly and inexpensively in case it needs repair. (If your bag is damaged by the airline, the airline will most likely be responsible for the claim. See p. 40.) When shopping, look for the construction details described in the following pages. Copy or cut out the luggage checklist at the end of this chapter and take it with you to the store when you shop for luggage.

Weight

Suitcases can weigh from about 6 pounds to over 11 pounds. Wheelaboards will weigh more than travel packs because of all the framing and hardware. Choose the lightest one that has all the features that you want and that you will be able to lift overhead when packed.

Color

Black is the hands-down favorite luggage color because it hides dirt, is inconspicuous, and looks classy. It is also more inconspicuous when traveling on the ground. However, if you plan to check your luggage often, there are so many black bags on the carousel or on buses and trains that a different color might enable you to spot your bag more easily. Red, burgundy, navy blue, and dark green are popular, with many lines introducing "designer" colors such as pink, bright green, or orange. Although the light colors may show more dirt and wear, you may like the change. In terms of security, it also makes it harder for someone to walk off with your bag and not be noticed! Whatever you take, personalize it in some way so that you recognize it easily.

Fabric

For maximum durability, select 1000-denier Cordura or 2500-denier ballistic nylon. These fabrics are sturdy enough to withstand abrasion and tearing with sharp objects. Moderate-use luggage may be made of 500 denier or 1800 denier polyester, a Cordura look-alike; these are not quite as tear or abrasion resistant but suffice when durability is not a priority issue. They are less expensive than Cordura or ballistic nylon, and for many travelers, do the trick. The 600 denier polyester doesn't hold up very well, and vinyl tends to crack or tear over time and should be avoided.

Other features that protect fabric from abrasion are plastic curb slides, found on the lower backside of the suitcase, and corner protectors. These add years of life to a bag.

Weatherproofing

Look for polyurethane coating (PUC) of at least 1 or $1^1/4$ ounces on the fabric to prevent moisture from drowning the bag. Other fabrics may have other treatments. Dye should not bleed when wet. Some bags have a Scotchgard Teflon coating on the outside for stain and soil resistance.

Handle

Look for comfortable carry handles, either a loop and flap design (two straplike handles joined with a small patch of leather) or single handle (like that on a standard suitcase). The handles should be riveted securely to the bag with strong hardware.

Retractable "telehandles" on rolling suitcases should be easy to open and close with one hand and lock into place in both the down and the up position. Locking in the down position can prevent damage resulting from the handle pulling out and being hit by something on the conveyor belt in the baggage handling system. Locking in the up position can mean that you can push or pull the bag without the handle succumbing to pressure. Some bags may have a two-position lock to adjust to the user's height. Some telehandles feature an ergonomic grip to relieve pressure on your hands and arms. Some luggage features recessed wells for the telehandle as well as zippered covers to protect the handle if checked through. Check for handle durability, and ask your retailer or manufacturer if the parts are readily available.

Frame/Wheel Assembly

On wheeled luggage, the frame and retractable handle and wheel assembly can be external or internal. An external assembly will, by necessity, result in the suitcase itself being a bit smaller, in order to allow the overall dimensions to conform to carry-on size guidelines. Additionally, external frames are more subject to damage if checked. Internally placed handles will give you added packing space, even though the bottom of the suitcase will not be flat (it will house the handle). You must weigh your decision based on your priorities—that is, how much you can get into the bag compared with other features that may be important to you. The frame, wheels, and handle assembly should be of the highest quality you can afford. My personal recommendation is to get the internal frame bag.

Wheels

Wheels maximize maneuverability and minimize damage to the bottom of the case. They are attached to frames with metal backplates and rivets or screws. They are sometimes retractable or removable.

Wheels should be of rubber urethane or in-line skate-wheel material. Make sure the hardware is securely fixed. Recessed wheels are less subject to damage than nonrecessed wheels. If the wheels are on the outside of the bag, make sure they are highly durable. Tutto luggage has highly durable nonrecessed wheels. There are bags with two-, three- and four-wheel systems.

Shoulder Strap

The shoulder strap takes a lot of stress and should have reinforced mounting areas and a wide, adjustable, and detachable strap. Look for strong hardware and a nonslip shoulder pad for comfort. Padded replacement shoulder straps are available in specialty travel stores and outdoor equipment stores.

Zippers

For maximum durability, choose nylon coil zippers or polyester coils. These are sturdy, work smoothly, and will not fail if a tooth breaks. Metal zippers have a greater tendency to jam or snag clothing; plastic is less sturdy than nylon. Choose zippers with two pull tabs that come together and close with a little combination or key lock. On semisoft bags, double zippers allow easy access even if the bag is stowed beneath the seat in front of you.

Stitching

Look for double stitching. Finished seams cost more money but will not fray.

Floor

The floor distributes the weight of the bag's contents and prevents sagging when the bag is lifted. Bags with structured floors are easier to pack. The floor also determines the way the bag is stored. Most semisoft bags have a padded cardboard or plastic insert to lend structure but allow the bag to be compressed when not in use. Rigid-framed bags have two types of floor. A rigid folding floor means that the floor is attached on only one side. When pressed into place, the bag has a rigid floor; when flipped up, the bag compresses for compact storage. A fixed floor means that the bag cannot be compressed when stored. Soft luggage has no floor reinforcement.

Special Features

Outside pockets make items easy to access. Flat pockets will hold papers and magazines, but do not expand. Expandable pockets give you room for more belongings, but also add inches to your carry-on when full, making them difficult to fit in overhead bins and lockers. However, they can be convenient on the ground. Bells and whistles such as packing systems, a hanger option, dividing mesh pockets, and wet-packs for wet and soiled garment are all available and must be decided upon. Just remember, the more additions a bag has inside, the less room you have to pack.

Luggage Carts

A luggage cart is a collapsible carrier that is ideal for pushing or pulling your luggage along concourses and streets and even up and down stairs. They are generally accepted aboard the aircraft *in addition* to carry-on luggage, and they are easily stowed. Many travelers find them indispensable. I strongly recommend a luggage cart if you are taking a heavy shoulder bag.

Carts can accommodate two or more pieces of luggage, making them appropriate for couples or families. You can use a luggage cart with your existing bag if you do not want to buy wheeled luggage. Used with a shoulder bag, they make luggage effortless to tow, adding immeasurably to your mobility. The best ones are easily collapsed and set up and come with sturdy wheels, step sliders, and a wide platform for added stability.

When choosing a luggage cart, assess your long-term needs and your travel lifestyle. If you travel light, buy a durable, high-quality lightweight cart, such as Remin's FliteLite C525. For long-term multipurpose use, when you are taking heavier loads or expect various types of surfaces, stairs, and curbs, invest in a heavier-duty cart, such as Remin's Concorde III, which has large wheels, a wide platform, and step sliders that ease going up and down curbs and stairs.

Remin Kart-a-Bag makes special models for salespeople who carry computers or sample cases, trade-show representatives who carry displays and materials, musicians, photographers, and numerous other mobile businesspeople. The company lends carts to its customers and offers a one-day turnaround on repairs.

Make sure you buy a durable luggage cart with unbreakable joints, heavy-duty telescoping tubing, and dependable wheels. It should have these features:

- Adequate carrying capacity—100 pounds is average for the smallest; some will carry up to 175 pounds
- The ability to remain upright when put down in a collapsed position
- A mechanism to lock it in place when upright so that luggage can be loaded and unloaded easily
- High-quality wheels, at least 3 inches in diameter, and 4 to 6 inches for added stability on staircases, curbs, or cobblestones
- An adequately wide base for multiple bags and added stability
- A size when folded that enables it to fit under the seat or overhead for storage
- A reasonable weight—between $3^1/2$ and 7 pounds (naturally, the heavier carts are more durable)
- Permanently attached elastic cords on the base
- Optional but highly desirable features include stair or curb slides ("step sliders") and a garment-bag attachment so that you can drape a dress or suit bag over your luggage.

Luggage Accessories

Here are some items you may need to purchase in addition to your luggage.

Identifier

A bright ribbon, tape, handle grip, or other unique identifier will distinguish your bag on the carousel if you check through.

Luggage Tags

Tags can fall off, so in addition to tags, label your luggage inside and out. For security reasons, use your name and business address and telephone number or your destination address and telephone number. In the event you check your bag, an itinerary placed in an outside pocket will help lost luggage reach you instead of being sent home.

Luggage Locks

All your luggage should lock. Use small locks for double-zippered suitcases. I recommend the combination type that you set yourself, as there are no keys to lose. If you plan on checking your luggage, use the special TSA-approved locks. They can be opened by inspectors and locked again after inspection. Some, such as the Sentry locks, alert you if your bag has indeed been opened (check contents immediately before you leave the airport).

TIP: Plastic cable ties make sturdy "locks" for your luggage. If one is cut off, you will notice immediately that your luggage has been opened. You can find cable ties in a variety of strengths and colors at any hardware store. Be sure to carry a blunt scissors so you can cut them off.

Retractable Luggage Lock

This is a steel cable lock with a combination that allows you to fasten your luggage to a park bench or other stationary object and allows you to take your eyes off the luggage. Some are specially made for laptop computers.

Replacement Padded Shoulder Straps

If your suitcase comes with a standard strap, purchase a more comfortable shoulder strap—Highly recommended!

Luggage Straps

These are nylon webbing straps, 1, 1$^1/_2$, or 2 inches wide, that wrap around the whole suitcase. They offer additional protection in transit. Some are lockable (TSA approved).

If You Check Your Luggage: Preventing Damage to Your Suitcases

Use Common Sense When Checking Luggage

- Check only luggage that is sturdy enough to withstand airline baggage-handling systems.

- Never check a bag that doesn't completely close. If you need a luggage strap or bungee cord to keep the bag closed, it probably won't survive the trip.

- Never check a bag that has broken components, such as wheels, handles, zippers, latches, and locks. Usually the airline insurance will not be required to cover damage to protruding elements such as handles, wheels, and straps.

- Never check a bag that is meant to be carried on. Most briefcases, tote bags, plastic garment covers, and items received through retail promotions are not designed to be checked luggage.

- Don't overpack. Overpacking puts a strain on zippers, seams, frames, and hinges.

- Clearly label luggage with your name, current address, and phone number. Be sure to put a business card or second label inside the bag in case your label is ripped off. If you are a member of an airline's frequent-flyer program, put your frequent-flyer number on a handwritten tag (available at the check-in counter) and attach it to the bag. You can even write your flight number, destination, and phone number on this tag. In the event that your baggage tag is ripped off, this can speed up delivery of your bag.

- Check your bag carefully in the luggage claim area before departing the airport.

- Check to see if it has been opened by security (there should be a note on it).

- Consider replacing old or worn luggage. Luggage that is several years old may not be able to withstand today's automated baggage-handling systems.

What To Do about Damaged Luggage

Before travel, check your airline's policy regarding damaged luggage and luggage theft.

Every airline states its policy on its website. Report any damage immediately to the baggage service center of the airline on which you traveled. File a damage claim before leaving the airport. Some airlines allow you to place a claim after you leave, but check with the airline before your flight. For example, Southwest required claims to be made within four hours of leaving the airport. Others may give you twenty-four hours. If you don't follow this procedure, you risk that the damage will not be covered under warranty or airline policy. Be prepared to negotiate politely with the airline representative, who wants to keep your business and has authority to solve most problems quickly and appropriately.

Have a Complaint about Damaged Luggage?
Contact

        www.dot.gov/consumer
        Aviation Consumer Protection Division
        U.S. Department of Transportation C-75
        400 7th St., SW, Room 4107
        Washington, D.C. 20590
        (202) 366-2220
        Email: airconsumer@ost.dot.gov

This checklist is useful in making comparisons among various items of luggage. When considering travel packs and wheeled bags, take the additional elements into consideration as well.

Luggage Buyer's Checklist: 45-inch Carry-on Bag

	Model 1	Model 2	Model 3	Model 4
Brand/name				
Store				
Price				
Weight				
Dimensions				
Volume				
Fabric				
Color				
Structured sides				
# of compartments	1 2 3	1 2 3	1 2 3	1 2 3
Pockets, outside				
Pockets, inside				
Handle				
Shoulder strap				
Zippers				
Tie straps				
Storage				
Other features				
Travel packs				
Zip-off daypack				
Internal frame				
Frameless				
Other features				
Wheeled bags				
Wheels, recessed or protruding				
Step sliders				
Handle, back or side				
Grab handle, side and/or top				
Other features				

Much of this information on luggage, courtesy of the Luggage and Leather Goods Manufacturers of America, now the Travel Goods Association, www.travel-goods.org.

3

TRAVEL GEAR

After choosing luggage, your next priority is putting together your travel gear: equipment and incidentals that you will need or want while away from home. Each item must be chosen carefully according to need, usefulness, weight, and size. Only pack essentials. Keep in mind that that there are literally hundreds of useful items, but if you take them all you will need three suitcases and a valet!

To cut down, find out what will be available at your destination. Share with a travel companion. Think of what you might find, improvise, or do without along the way. In choosing gear, think miniature. Scout backpacking stores, travel stores, and drug stores for compact and lightweight models.

When making your packing list, think first of the essentials—gear related to your safety, health, and hygiene—that will serve daily use. These are basics and generally do not change from trip to trip. Examples would be your toothbrush, toothpaste, floss, a travel alarm, a flashlight, a security wallet, sunscreen and hat, all-purpose travel soap, a water bottle, stain treatment, and a small sewing kit. For me, this also includes items that it would cause great inconvenience to be without in case of an emergency or at night when stores are closed, such as an eyeglass-repair kit, a first-aid kit (including Alka-Seltzer, Pepto-Bismol, ibuprofen, and adhesive bandages), and a nightlight.

Essentials also include any gear that is directly related to the climate and your activities, such as camera equipment for a safari, binoculars for viewing wildlife, insect repellent and mosquito netting for the tropics, or raingear and a travel umbrella for a European tour.

Next, add items that you simply must have to make you a happy traveler. These vary from person to person, from true minimalists who figure they can "make do" or improvise along the way to others who might feel that these items make the difference between a good trip and a great trip. These can be an inflatable pillow, a personal MP3 player, a white-noise machine, a small coffee maker or immersion heater, a hairdryer, or even a musical instrument! Keep in mind that it is you who will do the lugging, so try to be conservative here and cut down somewhere else.

Finally, there is gear for the "self-sufficient traveler." This person might bring a small tablecloth, a picnic kit, a towel, sleep-sheets, a tool kit, or office supplies. A woman alone might carry a hotel intruder alarm.

Use the following checklists to help organize your list and give you ideas. Then complete your list and go back over it with a critical eye. Try to eliminate as much as possible. If you think you'll bring it "just in case," leave it out. Then take out some more!

Be ruthless.

At the end of your trip, look at your list again. Note items that you overpacked and items that you wished you had brought. Save the list for your next trip, and you'll be on your way to being a very efficient packer.

The Bare Essentials Checklist

This list contains items that can become necessary on any trip and provide a minimum level of self-sufficiency. For annotated lists, read further on in this chapter. For basic lists, see the Quicklists in Appendix 4.

- [ ] security wallet (for contents, see pp. 48–49)

- [ ] travel alarm (watch, clock, or cell phone)

- [ ] travel lock

- [ ] toiletry kit: toothbrush with cap, toothpaste, dental floss, antiperspirant, all-purpose travel soap, shampoo/conditioner, sunscreen, lip balm, moisturizer, safety razor, shaving oil, nail clipper, comb or folding brush, sanitary items, birth control, toilet seat covers, tissue pack, moist towelettes

- [ ] eye care supplies: prescription glasses, sunglasses (in lightweight cases or wrapped in a bandanna), lens cleaner pads, contact lenses and supplies, eyeglass-repair kit

- [ ] medical kit: prescription medicines, antacid, diarrhea medicine, pain/fever reliever, cold pills, jet lag remedy, and so on

- [ ] first-aid kit: bandages, antiseptic wipes, blister kit, tweezers, insect repellent, anti-itch remedy, and so on

- [ ] clothing care kit: sewing kit, travel soap or detergent, clothesline, inflatable hanger, stain remedy, strong clips, sink stopper

- [ ] flashlight with extra battery and bulb

- [ ] water bottle, purifier if needed, snack

- [ ] notebook and pens, highlighter

- [ ] small camera, film or memory cards, batteries

- [ ] rain protection: hat, small umbrella, packable raincoat

- [ ] swim supplies: goggles, ear and nose plugs as needed

- [ ] earplugs (for noise protection)

- [ ] plastic bags, various sizes for wet and soiled items, organizing

- [ ] fold-up nylon expandable bag

- [ ] technology as desired: cell phone, computer, MP3 player/iPod

- [ ] lightweight book
- [ ] sleepsheet (for hostel)

Security Wallets

Your first consideration is your method of carrying valuables. I urge you to take a security wallet, which is a secure, close-to-the-body pouch available in various designs, to be worn underneath your clothes (different vendors call various models *security wallet, money pouch, neck pouch,* or *money belt*). The security wallet will carry your passport, money, traveler's checks, credit cards, airline tickets, and an extra copy of your eyeglass and medication prescriptions. Never put your valuables in a wallet, waistpack, daypack, purse, carry-on, or checked luggage. These are suitable for a bit of cash for the day, but not for the bulk of your resources. Valuables should go on your person, hidden underneath your clothes. Select clothing that will accommodate the security wallet; assume that you will be wearing it all the time. Even if you are sure you are going to a "safe" area, take one along for peace of mind.

In selecting a security wallet, consider weather resistance, the type of clothing you will be wearing, and how you want to wear the wallet—around your waist, under your shoulder, around your leg, or, as a comfortable hanging wallet, tucked along your thigh like a pocket. I prefer multipurpose styles such as the World Class Passport Carrier and the Eagle Creek Undercover Security Wallet that can be moved around depending on what you are wearing. I don't like those with neck straps because these invite trouble and they are bulky. Materials should be weather resistant. If you are going to tropical climates, choose a cotton- or Cambrelle-backed money pouch—it will be cooler than nylon—or use one that hangs like a pocket.

World Class Passport Carrier

This versatile wallet can be worn with all styles of clothing. It can be used as a hanging loop wallet, a money belt around your waist, or as a shoulder holster. The loop has a steel cable running through it. The detachable, adjustable strap also has a steel cable inside so that it cannot easily be cut off. The nylon pouch has three sections: the front section has a pocket for an American passport and credit cards; the middle zippered section will hold cash and traveler's checks (the money is thus invisible when you need to pull out only your passport at a checkpoint or bank); the rear compartment has room for tickets and other documents. Other nice features include a diagonal zipper, which prevents the contents from falling out, and a polyurethane coating for weather resistance. There are no external seams to fray or tear. There are two sizes available, allowing for variation in ticket quantity and size.

The most comfortable, coolest, and most accessible way to wear a security wallet is to fasten it to your belt or strap it around your waist and then tuck it down your skirt, slacks, or shorts. When you need something in it, pull it up and out, and tuck it back—it remains attached to you at all times.

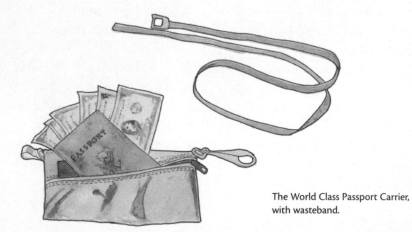

The World Class Passport Carrier, with wasteband.

Around-the-Waist Security Wallets

These rectangular money pouches will hold a passport, money, and tickets. I personally do not recommend them for hot weather because they sit across the stomach or abdomen and can be uncomfortable (although when made of cotton they are better), but many people prefer them. Eagle Creek makes a nice line with a Cambrelle fabric backing that is more absorbent than cotton and dries much faster.

Neck Pouches

This is one of my favorite kinds of wallet because it is easily tucked beneath unbelted skirts as well as slacks and shorts. Unlike the rather bulky around-the-waist security wallet described above, this model is a vertical pouch attached to a long, adjustable strap. It looks like it should be worn hung around the neck, so that the pouch hangs down over the chest. But I find that to be bulky and less secure, because the neck strap can remain visible and tempt predators. The best way to wear a neck pouch is actually with the strap around your waist so that the pouch hangs vertically on your hip like a pocket and is tucked underneath your clothes. This method is cool and compact. The Undercover Security Wallet by Eagle Creek is a great model because it has an outside zippered flap that makes retrieval of a little cash or a credit card easy without taking out the entire pouch. Another way to wear it is on your shoulder, with the pouch close to your body under your arm.

Shoulder Holsters

Though they make access more difficult, shoulder holsters are generally favored by men. Be sure to wear them under your shirt, not just under your jacket.

Leg Pouches

These come in leather or elasticized nylon spandex and fit around the calf or ankle.

Money Belts

These conventional-looking belts have a zippered compartment on the inside for storing folded cash and documents. (Wrap these in plastic to protect from moisture.) They come in woven fabric or leather.

Watertight Pouches

These convenient, watertight security wallets can be worn around your waist while you are swimming. They are useful for carrying your valuables at the beach or pool. Eagle Creek and Cascade Seal Pack make good ones.

Clothing with Pockets

Many specially designed travel clothes feature sewn-in security pockets. Among other manufacturers, Norm Thompson and Orvis make blazers with concealed pockets. Christine Columbus offers a women's half-slip with hidden pockets on the hem. (See appendix 2, Resources.)

Money and Travel Documents

These items should be stowed in your security wallet. Pack, *as applicable*:

☐ passport, photo ID, driver's license, birth certificate

☐ cash, foreign currency

☐ credit cards (one or two)

☐ ATM card

- [ ] checks (one or two)
- [ ] prepaid telephone card
- [ ] traveler's checks (half in your money belt, half in your daypack or bag)
- [ ] traveler's check record
- [ ] list of any PIN and calling-card access codes you need to remember
- [ ] auto club card
- [ ] 3 x 5 card with emergency phone numbers (including main home contact, a twenty-four-hour travel agent, medical and auto insurance, U.S. embassies and consulates, and doctors at your destination); include medical history/list of allergies and the like (see appendix 4 for details). *Do not put your social security or credit card numbers on this card.*
- [ ] medicine and eyeglass or contact lens prescriptions
- [ ] list of addresses
- [ ] student ID card or hostel pass
- [ ] train pass or voucher
- [ ] visa(s), extra passport photos
- [ ] other _____

Accessible Cash

Pack the following in an accessible wallet or, better yet, a brightly colored, flat-zippered nylon organizer pouch about 5 x 7 inches in size. This will serve for daily access.

- [ ] cash and tip money—enough for the day only
- [ ] traveler's check
- [ ] coins
- [ ] receipts, ticket stubs, and other "collectibles"

Other Documents

In your suitcase, store an envelope with photocopies of important documents (see below) as well as internet vouchers and tickets and any other papers and photographs you might want. I normally take one 9 x 12 manila envelope for this purpose, or I use several plastic #10 envelopes and organize contents sequentially according to when I need them on the trip.

For maximum safety, copies of all of the following information should also be with a home contact person. Keep that person's phone number in your security wallet. In case of theft, you can call your contact to cancel your cards and send you anything you need.

☐ copy of passport (all pages)

☐ airline, bus, and train tickets (photocopy tickets in case they get lost)

☐ itinerary

☐ vouchers and confirmations

☐ trip cancellation policy

☐ phone number of ground transportation provider

☐ other half of your traveler's checks

☐ traveler's checks record

☐ PIN and phone-card access codes

☐ medical, auto, and travel insurance papers

☐ sales receipts for any equipment to be declared at customs

☐ customs declaration papers

☐ copies of medical and eyeglass or contact lens prescriptions

☐ immunization certificate

☐ health forms, list of allergies, medical history, special medications

☐ list of gifts and sizes

☐ other _____

Online Internet Document Storage

The Internet is the light traveler's best friend! Instead of carrying lots of paper copies with you, you can store copies of all the above documents online at Lonely Planet's Travel Vault. The site uses commercial-grade encryption to keep your information super secure. Only you have access to it via a personalized password. You can access the documents 24/7 from anywhere you have internet access. LP's service also features many other global communications benefits. Check out www.lonelyplanet.ekit.com.

Another option is to carry a USB memory stick (sometimes called a flash drive) with your info. A memory stick is a backup data disk that is small enough to carry in your security wallet, on a keychain, or in your purse. To retrieve the information, you can plug it into any computer that has a USB port.

A commercial product called Critical Access provides the software to enter all your emergency information, health records, medical images, surgeries, and so on into one flash drive. Visit www.protravelgear.com.

Yet another possibility is to buy a larger, higher capacity portable hard drive that can be plugged in via USB or a FireWire cable. These devices are excellent for backup at home as well as on the road. Ask your computer dealer to recommend a device similar to the hard drive on your computer.

Organizing Your Toiletries and Incidentals

Make little kits to organize your personal items. For example, assemble all your toiletries in one kit and make up others for medical needs, clothing care, first aid, office supplies, bedside needs, picnicking, and so on. I like to make an in-flight kit so I can pull it out easily on the plane.

I find that the most time-consuming and easy-to-forget items to pack in a rush are the little toiletry items. If you can, always keep your kits replenished and filled at home, or pack them well in advance of your trip. You will be amazed how this cuts down on the stress come packing time, and you'll always be ready to go should a wonderfully unexpected trip come along!

The following packing supplies will be helpful.

Organizer Bags and Pouches for Toiletries and Incidentals

Small unstructured kits allow the most flexibility in using packing space, compared with the traditional boxy shaving kits or a large hanging toiletry organizer. They are also easy to transport out of the bag to the location where they will be used in your room. Clear or brightly colored pouches in different colors provide color coding, which makes kits easy to find and their contents known at a glance. It is also handy if the pouch can stand up on its own, using less space on the counter. Always choose the smallest pouch or organizer that will hold what you need. You can use plastic bags in various sizes (the heavier "freezer" quart and gallon sizes are handiest), colored nylon pouches, or any type of unstructured, lightweight, packable organizer or toiletry kit. Hanging models such as those made by Eagle Creek and L.L.Bean are great for outdoor use or very tight quarters—if the organizational pockets work for you, great! I like water-repellent, zippered nylon pouches such as those made by Outdoor Research, Eagle Creek, and Victorinox. Adventure Medical Kits makes Clear Pockets, which have a vinyl window so you can see and locate items easily. Mesh pouches can be used for dry items.

Another option is to use the new multisized "packing cubes," which are modular shapped pouches. They are meant to fit in modular fashion in your suitcase. Although not necessary, they are a fun and handy packing aid and use the space well.

Organizer pouches can also be used for items such as underwear, socks, or any rolled items. If you like these, use them! Another idea is the super-lightweight Sea to Summit Ultra-Sil Dry Sack—a water-proof stuff sack that comes in many sizes (REI). Stuff sacks can be useful for travel packs. All stuff sacks and pouches should be treated on the inside for water repellency, so they can be used for wet and soiled items.

Plastic Bottles

Transfer any products from large containers into high quality 1-ounce, 2-ounce, and 4-ounce plastic bottles, such as Nalgene, available at good outdoor and travel stores. Bottles with screw-on caps are best. To find out how much you might need, track your consumption before your trip. (Do not forget to take enough contact lens solution—it may be hard to find on the road.) To prevent leaks, leave half an inch of air space at the top of each bottle. Squeeze out the air and close the bottle to create a vacuum. You can also tape the tops and store the bottles in a resealable bag. If you don't want to bother with all the pouring and sealing, you can buy trial- and travel-sized products at most drug stores.

Additional Packing Aids

These are "nice-to-have" but not "must-have" accessories. Some do add quite a bit of expense to your packing investment.

Shirt Folders

These relatively new innovations by Eagle Creek are fabric envelopes with a stiff folding board inside in which you can fold and stack shirts compactly. (There are other brands on the market now too.) These folders are *not* required for my Bundle Method of packing, but if you like them, they can be accommodated. Keep in mind that the shirts may be creased at the folds when you unpack them. The folders come in different sizes. I like the medium size.

Shoe Bags and Covers

These are handy for keeping shoes clean and separate from other items. Some models are water repellant to shield clothing from moisture and dirt. For high heels you can also wrap tissue paper around the heels so they don't snag clothing.

Plastic Compression Bags

These are another recent invention that are meant to compress bulky garments so that they can be packed flat in a minimal amount of space. They are useful for such items as down and fleece jackets. Compression bags are sturdy plastic zip locking bags that come in a variety of sizes for packing. They are made with a special valve at the bottom that lets air out but not in. You insert a folded garment, then zip-lock the bag and roll it up, beginning at the zippered end, pressing the air out. The result is a "vacuum-sealed" garment. These can be very useful, but if you are dependant on them, take extra bags. They can fail, and you can be left with a garment that is too bulky to pack and must be dragged along.

Envelopes

Since many trips are now planned over the Internet, tickets and confirmations are printed at home and need to be carried along. For this purpose I like clear, colored plastic business size envelopes, found in office supply stores. I take several and label each according to segments or aspects of my trip. For example, pink might be airline, car, and hotel reservations; blue might be "Paris," green might be "Italy," and so on. I carry these in my day bag, and make sure I have copies elsewhere (with a home contact and in a companion's suitcase). These envelopes are reusable and come in handy for stubs, receipts, and so on.

Manila envelopes measuring 9 x 12 or 10 x 13 inches are useful for sending home brochures, organizing guidebook pages, travel notes, and so on. Preaddress them! Tyvek envelopes are even lighter than paper and are moisture resistant.

Travel Jewelry Bag (Optional)

Keep it lightweight and simple.

Health and Comfort

What follows is a checklist for items that will keep you comfortable and healthy as you travel. (Details on many of the items follow the checklist.) Think about each one in view of your destination, mode of travel, and personal needs. Remember, each item adds bulk and weight to your bag, which you will have to carry! Ready-made travel-sized first-aid, blister care, and dental kits are widely available from outdoor and travel stores and websites.

Medical Needs

☐ two complete sets of prescription medicine in small bottles, one for your day bag and one for your main bag

☐ a 3 x 5-inch card with your doctor's name and number, your medical history, and a list of allergies (or have this information on your personal technology)

☐ insulated bag for medicine, if needed

☐ nonprescription medications (such as acetaminophen, aspirin, ibuprofen, antacid, anti-diarrheal, laxative, antihistamine, decongestant tablets, cold or flu relief, throat lozenges, fungus treatment cream, vitamins, sleeping pills)

☐ collapsible drinking cup

☐ other _____

Eye Care

☐ glasses, sunglasses, cases (or wrap in bandanna)

☐ your most-recently replaced pair of glasses as a backup (optional)

☐ eyeglass-repair kit

☐ contact lenses/case (take extra lenses)

- [ ] contact lens kit or sterilizer
- [ ] contact lens solution

Outdoor Protection

- [ ] sunscreen
- [ ] aloe vera or Solarcaine for sunburns
- [ ] lip balm
- [ ] hat, visor, or bandanna
- [ ] insect repellent
- [ ] hydrocortisone cream (1%) or anti-itch balm
- [ ] mosquito netting, if needed

Food and Water

- [ ] water bottle or flask
- [ ] energy snacks (energy bars, trail mix, crackers, fruit, candy, jerky, gum)
- [ ] water-purification equipment or tablets, if needed

Travel Comfort Kit

- [ ] jet-lag remedy
- [ ] motion-sickness medication or aid
- [ ] remedy for ear discomfort during takeoff and landing
- [ ] ear plugs
- [ ] eyeshades
- [ ] travel pillow
- [ ] travel compression socks
- [ ] spritz bottle or facial mister

☐ eye wash

☐ personal items: comb, lipstick or balm, facial-cleansing pads, moisturizer, sanitary items, moist towelettes, safety razor, and so on

☐ other _____

Insect Repellent and Mosquito Netting

Insect protection can range from simply preventing bites to preventing malaria in many areas of the world. N, N-Diethyl-*m*-toluamide, marketed as DEET, is the main chemical ingredient in insect repellents, which vary in strength and come as sprays, liquids, or solid roll-ons. Those containing 12 percent to a maximum of 35 percent DEET are recommended. Choose a low-percentage variety for children.

If you do not want to use a chemical, try natural products such as citronella and eucalyptus. These are quite popular and very effective. If you are going to a malaria-infested destination, take repellent and mosquito netting or headnet (some are treated with added repellents), and consider the insect-repellent clothing (such as BUZZ OFF) clothing that offers complete coverage. Also find out what vaccinations you need from your physician or the Centers for Disease Control, and get the shots six to eight weeks before you leave, since some require a series.

Water Bottle or Flask

Remaining hydrated keeps you energetic and healthy as your body undergoes the stress of new environments, especially hot or dry ones. The smallest flask should hold at least 6 ounces; the largest, up to 1 liter. You can buy screw-top commercial water bottles, or buy a reusable water bottle. Collapsible plastic pouches allow for easy packing and carrying. The Flexi Flask is even boilable for water purification. If you plan to take drink mixes or prepare purified water, get a wide-mouthed water bottle. I especially like tote bags and daypacks that feature a water bottle holder on the outside. The Solutions catalog sells a Cordura nylon bottle carrier with

Velcro straps to attach securely to the retractable handle of your wheelaboard (see appendix 2, Resources).

Another option is the Camelback hydration pack, found at outdoor stores. This is a collapsible plastic bag that can be worn on your back, and you can drink water through a connected tube as your move. There are many models—the UnBottle model can be put into any day- or backpack. Be sure to bring the (very small) cleaning tools and disinfectant to keep it clean.

Water-Purification Equipment

Traveler's diarrhea, hepatitis A, cholera, shigella, giardia, and salmonella can all be contracted by drinking the local water supply in many countries. To protect yourself, make sure you have some form of water purification with you. For emergency purposes, carry Potable Aqua or some other iodine-based, chlorine-free tablet that comes in a small bottle. Add one tablet (two if giardia is suspected) to 1 quart or liter of water, wait three minutes, shake the bottle, and wait ten more minutes before drinking the water (for giardia protection, wait twenty minutes). Designed for emergencies, iodine should not be used on a continuous basis.

The Steripen, a lightweight, easy-to-hold portable device (6.5 ounces and 7.6 x 1.5 inches), conveniently provides safe drinking water for repeated use. Steripen uses an ultraviolet light to destroy waterborne microbes. This is fundamentally the same technology used in water-treatment plants, but miniaturized! Steripen eliminates viruses, bacteria, and protozoa, including giardia and cryptosporidium. Simply insert the Steripen UV lamp in a bottle of 16 or 32 ounces of water and agitate for up to ninety seconds, and you have chemical-free, safe water. It can be used with clear, fresh outdoor water sources and with tap water. If the water is unclear, you need an additional filter that fits on the wide mouth of a Nalgene water bottle to filter the water before purification. The pen takes four AA batteries—alkaline, lithium, or NiMH rechargeables; the number of doses varies by type of battery used. At about $150, it is pricey but can make a huge difference when traveling in areas with questionable water sources. For complete information visit www. hydro-photon.com. Steripen is available at many travel stores.

Other types of portable purifiers include the PUR Voyageur, which provides the highest level of protection and is still portable enough to pack easily. The purifier is an 11-ounce cylindrical pump, 6½ inches long and 2 inches wide, which processes up to 1 liter per minute. A replaceable carbon cartridge removes chemicals and unpleasant tastes. The cartridge lasts for 100 gallons, or 1,600 cups of water.

Other manufacturers of good travel-size water purification systems are Katadyn (the Hiker), Sweetwater, and First Need. Check out these and others at outdoor and camping stores.

The Katadyn Micro Filter Bottle is an 18-ounce plastic sport bottle that holds a special filter in its cap. You simply fill the bottle, replace the cap, and drink. This bottle fills from any water supply and removes giardia, cryptosporidium, viruses, chlorine, lead, and heavy metals. It also comes in a model from which you drink with a straw. The filter processes 1,800 refills, or 300 gallons, before you need a replacement filter. This is great for at home, for daily or emergency use, as well as travel.

All of these purifiers are approved by the USEPA.

Don't forget, as a last resort you can always boil water for twenty minutes if you have the opportunity.

Jet-Lag Remedy

If you've ever suffered from the effects of jet lag, you should know about this new product. Originally developed in New Zealand, No-Jet-Lag is a unique homeopathic remedy constituted of natural herbs that alleviates the symptoms of jet lag. Its effectiveness had been clinically proven and is recognized internationally by business travelers, sports teams, tour operators, and airline personnel. I always use this product myself and have arrived alert both at destination and at home.

NOTE: The makers of No-Jet-Lag make a whole line of homeopathic remedies. Look for them at online travel suppliers.

Motion-Sickness Remedy

There are several kinds. Besides medication, you can buy Sea Bands, elasticized wristbands that have a hard plastic bump. When the bands are placed snugly on the wrist, the bump presses an acupressure point that controls balance and nausea. Both wristbands must be worn. People who use these bands swear by them. The makers of No-Jet-Lag also make a homeopathic motion-sickness remedy.

Ear-Pressure Remedy

Many travelers experience ear discomfort during takeoffs and landings. If you have a cold, allergies, or a sinus condition, the pain is exacerbated. EarPlanes disposable earplugs reduce the pain. These plugs have a hole in them and a CeramX filter. They are simply inserted into the ears before takeoff and removed when the airplane arrives at the gate and the cabin door is opened. They are available in adult and children's sizes.

Comfort Needs

When you are traveling, rest and sleep are necessities, not luxuries. Consider items like travel pillows carefully, even if they seem like "extras."

Travel Pillow, Eyeshade

Your own travel pillow will help you sleep in any hotel room, campground, train, or bus. Look for a durable, washable one. Crescentshaped, inflatable neck pillows with washable cozy covers are made by Eagle Creek and Travel Komfort Kollar. Down and feather versions can be bought at outdoor stores. Although it takes up a lot of space, the fleece-covered Bucky Pillow is incredible—it feels like a pillow and a teddy bear rolled into one.

Travel Compression Socks

The gradual compression design of TravelSox helps stimulate blood flow and in turn reduces swelling in your legs and feet. They are helpful if you are confined to an airline seat, are on your feet all day, suffer from circulation problems, are pregnant, or simply want to feel more energized. They have 300 percent more elasticity than similar leg wear and are made of moisture-wicking Coolmax.

Ear Plugs
Ear plugs are invaluable if you land in a noisy hotel. A good brand is the foam-type E.A.R. If you are extraordinarily sensitive to noise, you might want to consider a Marsona Sound Conditioner. This small electronic device drowns out background noise with the soothing sounds of rain or a waterfall. It comes in single or dual voltages and weighs about a pound. This is unquestionably a luxury for most of us, but it might be indispensable for some people.

Personal Air Purifier
This mini device ($1^{1}/_{2}$ ounces) hangs around your neck and helps to purify your breathing space by processing air with "advanced plasma discharge design." (www.ProTravelGear.com).

Collapsible Travel Seat
If you think you might need to sit down at any time, you can tote a portable seat anywhere. Models include the Easy Going Sport Seat and the Tri-Lite Folding Stool (available at Easygoing.com and REI, respectively). Also found at stores that feature camping equipment.

First-Aid/Health Kit
First-aid kits are very personal and differ by individual, destination, and level of protection desired. The following are basic suggestions for general travel. Excellent ready-made first-aid kits for travelers are assembled by Adventure Medical Kits, Atwater Carey, Ltd., and Outdoor Research (physician owned). These are available at travel and outdoor stores.

The following kit will handle most minor health problems:

☐ medical items from Medical Needs list (see p. 55)

☐ bandages, various sizes

☐ antiseptic pads

- [ ] hydrocortisone cream for bites, cuts, sunburns
- [ ] tweezers
- [ ] moleskin or Spenco 2nd Skin (a medicated aerosol)
- [ ] other _____

Consider these additional items for maximum protection:

- [ ] emergency dental kit (see appendix 2, Resources)
- [ ] emergency first-aid handbook (pocketed)
- [ ] gauze bandages and pads, surgical tape
- [ ] small blunt scissors
- [ ] thermometer (digital)
- [ ] latex gloves (or nitrile or other nonlatex, if allergic to latex)
- [ ] ace bandage with clips
- [ ] hot/cold compress
- [ ] emergency blanket
- [ ] personal syringe kit
- [ ] other _____

Toiletries/Personal Items

Choose toiletries carefully, and keep in mind that many items will be available at your destination.

I can't say enough about the new travel towels that have been developed in recent years. They are much more useful that ordinary terrycloth towels. There are a few types. Packtowl makes one of chamois-like viscose that can hold up to ten times its weight in moisture. Compact and lightweight, it works equally well damp or dry. This quick-drying towel does not fray or pill and is machine- or hand-washable. You can use it as a washcloth or towel; as a dish cloth, sponge, potholder, or napkin; or as a headband or dust mask.

It is also useful as an emergency compress, bandage, or tourniquet; as an ankle or splint wrap; or as a marker or flag. I have cut one up into small washcloths and kept them damp in a zip-locking bag to use instead of moist towelettes. If you're traveling with kids, they are invaluable. They come in three sizes: standard, the middle-sized Aquatowl, and the bath-sized Megatowl.

Microfiber towels are also widely available. These have a thinner, more pliable feel. They come in all sizes, from washcloths to large towels. They are available from many manufacturers, including Cascade Packtowl, REI, Eagle Creek, and Rick Steves.

Bandannas are also useful, as are large handkerchiefs.

Keep your makeup to a minimum by choosing small sample and travel-sized containers. Look for compact innovations such as eye-makeup-remover swabs, beauty tools in a compact case, or blush, shadow, and lipstick in a small case. Take a small pocket mirror, such as a compact lighted mirror that can stand up or be used as a compact. Also, keep makeup choices to a minimum—making do with eyeliner or shadow, mascara, and lip gloss is ideal. Or take a vacation from makeup!

TIP: If you will be in a hot climate, take lip pencils. Unlike lipsticks, they do not melt.

Leave personal appliances such as hairdryers home if at all possible, because they are bulky. Consider an easy-care haircut instead! Your hotel may provide a dryer; call ahead to check availability. (For more on electrical appliances, see p. 80.) If you must take a dryer, for international travel take a small, dual-voltage dryer with adapters or a single-voltage model with a high-wattage converter and adapters. If you need a curling iron, take one that uses butane, or a dual-voltage iron with adapters for international travel.

NOTE: Butane cartridge *refills* cannot be carried aboard a plane.

It never hurts to carry a small roll of toilet paper or a packet of tissues with you, and I've been in places where, thank goodness, I had seat covers. Foil-wrapped moist towelettes, baby wipes, antibacterial wipes, and so on can be helpful, especially if you are traveling with children. Feminine sanitary products are available worldwide, but U.S. brands are very expensive when purchased abroad. If you don't want to pay extra, take enough tampons or sanitary napkins with you for the entire trip. The O.B. brand tampon without applicator is compact. Women can use panty liners in underwear to cut down on laundry. Or try the nondisposable varieties that are available.

Women traveling abroad or camping may want to consider bringing a urinary director device. Freshette is a palm-sized, reusable, lightweight plastic device that enables women to urinate while standing or sitting with minimal undressing. It is available at Easy Going, REI, and other outdoor stores, or direct from the manufacturer (www.freshette.com).

Here is a fairly complete list of options. For light travel, take only the essentials.

☐ multipurpose travel soap (can be used as shampoo too)

☐ shampoo and conditioner (try two-in-one brands), other hair products

☐ facial cleansing pads (disposable)

☐ moisturizer

☐ antiperspirant

☐ dental supplies: toothbrush with cap or holder, toothpaste, dental floss, mouthwash, dentures, orthodontic appliances, case

☐ shaving supplies: safety shaver, electric shaver, shaving cream or oil, aftershave, styptic pencil

☐ hair supplies: comb, folding hairbrush, clips, hair ties, curling iron, hair dryer, and so on

☐ manicure items: nail clipper, file, polish, polish remover pads

☐ compact mirror

☐ clear nail polish (for runs in nylons)

☐ fast-drying travel towel and washcloth

Hygiene Supplies

- ☐ toilet paper and seat covers
- ☐ moist towelette packets or antibacterial gel
- ☐ feminine sanitary items
- ☐ Freshette (see above)
- ☐ personal _____
- ☐ other _____

Shoe and Foot Care

- ☐ foot cream
- ☐ moleskin or Spenco 2nd Skin
- ☐ foot powder
- ☐ removable insoles and other shoe supplies
- ☐ other _____

Repair Kit

- ☐ tiny roll of duct tape, patch kit for pack/sleeping bag, and so on
- ☐ a film canister filled with safety pins, nails, screws, and so on
- ☐ pocket knife or multiuse tool (must be checked through or bought at destination)
- ☐ repair supplies for your pack or other equipment

Room and Security

Do not depend on the hotel's wake-up call. Bring a compact clock that is easy to see at night and easily set. I like bright-colored models (such as red, yellow, or white) because they are less likely to be forgotten in the hotel room (L.L.Bean has cute ones in five colors). For more on security, see chapter 11.

- [ ] travel alarm (clock, cell phone, or wristwatch with alarm)
- [ ] small, sturdy flashlight (with extra batteries and bulb for long trips)
- [ ] headlamp or other hands-free flashlight
- [ ] night light, fluorescent tape for marking light switches, or light-sticks (good for brownouts or blackout)
- [ ] portable door lock or rubber doorstop
- [ ] portable hands-free reading light with extra batteries and bulb
- [ ] intruder alarm
- [ ] portable smoke alarm
- [ ] extension cord
- [ ] silky sheets or sleep sheets for youth hostels (if needed)
- [ ] Pac-safe, a portable, packable slash-proof bag lined with eXomesh wire mesh (see the next section, Security for Your Belongings)
- [ ] Pac-safe wire mesh security wrap for your travel pack
- [ ] other _____

Security for Your Belongings

Several types of products are available to protect your belongings. This is particularly important in places where stealing and slashing is an issue.

Pac-Safe products are constructed from eXomesh, a high-tensile, flexible stainless-steel wire mesh laminated between layers of durable, weather-resistant nylon. This fabric is used to make several handy items. One is the Travel Safe, a bag with a steel cable attached to it so that you can anchor it in the hotel room or your car trunk, or to your luggage. It is big enough for cameras, wallets, and other valuables.

Pac-Safe also makes a daypack and a waistpack-shoulderpouch combo bag.

Finally, they offer a full-size wire-mesh casing that wraps around your travelpack but is collapsible to a very small size.

Clothing Care

By picking packable fabrics and using the Bundle Method of packing (see chapter 6) and other wrinkle-removal methods (see pp. 109–111), you can leave your travel iron or steamer at home. Take one only if you want extra insurance against wrinkles. Make sure it is dual voltage for international travel.

A steamer is a plastic vessel with a heating element inside. You fill it with water (in some a bit of salt must be added to speed the steaming), plug it in, and in about five minutes you will have a supply of hot steam that lasts between eight and twelve minutes. Hang up your garment and glide the steamer along to coax the wrinkles out. Steamers are wonderful for removing travel wrinkles in light- and medium-weight fabrics. They weigh much less than irons do, and you can hang the garment up anywhere to steam it. Steamers cannot, however, set a crease in slacks or put the crispness back into a skirt, shirt, or jacket. To do this you need the weight and heat provided by an iron. Do not expect the same performance from a travel iron as you get from your iron at home. It lacks the weight and heating ability. Still, high-quality models will work well on the road.

Some works-in-a-pinch alternatives to these appliances are Wrinkle Free and Lewis N Clark Wrinkle Remover—sprays that act as fabric relaxers on all fabrics except 100 percent polyester and silk. You spray the garment and use your hand to smooth out wrinkles.

You can buy a tiny sewing kit, or assemble one in a clear plastic film canister. Include needles, straight pins inserted into a small piece of fabric, thread wrapped around a small piece of cardboard, a thimble, several sizes of safety pins, and some basic buttons. Before you go on a trip, you can reinforce the stitching on buttons and sew an extra button on the inside of each garment. A small roll of Scotch or duct tape will make an emergency hem.

If you plan to hand wash clothes on your trip, you will want to bring some or all of the laundry items on the list that follows. For tips on cleaning clothes while traveling (and explanations for some of these items), see pages 108–111.

Multipurpose travel soap or detergent is sold as a liquid in a squeeze bottle, in dry packets, or as a solid. You'll find it in travel and outdoor stores. For a clothesline, take the elasticized braided Flexo-line, which does not need clips to hang most items, a bungee-style line with hooks, or 10 feet of nylon cord. Take one or two inflatable hangers for drying blouses and delicates quickly. A couple of strong clips, such as vinyl-coated spring clips, are handy, as are the laundry clips with a hanger option. A sink stopper—the flat, round type—can be helpful; these are often missing from sinks and tubs. For a laundry sack, you can use a plastic bag, a mesh laundry bag, or your fold-up nylon bag!

Stain Removal

Part of maintaining your clothes on the road is dealing with the inevitable stains acquired while picnicking, in restaurants, and in general activity. Before you start trying to remove a stain, make sure you know what kind of fabric you are working with and what caused the stain. Check the clothing tag; some stain-removal agents should not be used on certain fabrics. Here are general procedures:

- Treat stains *immediately, before they set*. Fresh stains are much easier to remove. Sponge or rinse with cool water or club soda.

- Take dry-cleanables in for professional treatment immediately if possible.

- Do not apply any heat—from hot water, an iron, or a dryer—until the stain has been removed. Heat will set most stains. Start with cold water, then go on to warm.

- First remove as much of the potential stain as possible by blotting, absorbing, or scraping off all excess liquid or solids.

- Test the garment for colorfastness by using the cleaning agent first on a hidden inside seam or the hem.

- Remove stains by blotting, flushing (applying liquid so it flows through the fabric), or rinsing, not by rubbing.

- Apply stain removers and rinsing liquid to the back of the stain. When applying, always work from the outside in to contain the stain.

- Rinsing a dry-cleanable item means sponge-rinsing with a wet clean cloth. Put a dry cloth on the opposite side to absorb excess water as you rinse. Never flush a dry-cleanable garment.

- To avoid leaving a ring, "feather" or blend the edges of the wet spot into the dry area after each rinse. Lightly wipe off with a lifting motion from the inside out.

If you want to be prepared for stains, take one of these.

For Washable Fabrics
A small solid stick or tube of liquid stain remover. Travel-sized products include Janie, Kiss Off, Magic Wand (good for ballpoint ink), EverCare Stain Eraser, Shout Wipes Plus towelettes, and Tide to Go Instant Stain Remover Pen.

Motsenbocker's Lift-Off Stain Remover (liquid, three bottles in travel-sized kit) will prepare you any kind of stain, from food to grease, adhesive, or ink.

These are great for family travel. They must all be laundered out.

For Dry Clean, Colorfast Fabrics, Including Silk and Wool
Janie Dry Stick (a chalk-like substance that absorbs) or packaged spot-remover pads (read the label instructions before using).

The following items will allow you to wash and maintain your wardrobe; you'll also be ready to make minor repairs and remove stains.

Basic Kit

- ☐ sewing kit
- ☐ multipurpose travel soap
- ☐ clothesline
- ☐ inflatable hanger
- ☐ hanger clips
- ☐ stain treatment product
- ☐ sink stopper
- ☐ plastic bag for carrying wet or soiled clothing

Optional Items

- ☐ travel towel (for blotting extra moisture)
- ☐ plastic skirt hanger
- ☐ detergent packets (dry)
- ☐ cold-water soap packets (dry)
- ☐ shoe-shine pads
- ☐ lint brush (or use Scotch tape)
- ☐ spray-on wrinkle remover
- ☐ travel iron or steamer (and salt if necessary)

Entertainment

These are extras that make travel a little more enjoyable. Take what you have room for. (See pp. 80–85 for advice on electronics.)

- [ ] lightweight book
- [ ] cards, travel games, variety puzzle magazine
- [ ] headphones
- [ ] personal radio, MP3 player/iPod, CD player (charger, accessories)
- [ ] computer, DVD player, DVDs
- [ ] electronic games, charger, smart cards, and the like
- [ ] travel or shortwave radio
- [ ] microcassette or digital recorder for recording lectures
- [ ] jump rope, inflatable beach ball, exercise bands
- [ ] musical instrument (ideally small!)
- [ ] other _____

Sightseeing and Photography

Guidebooks and maps greatly enhance a trip—but paper is heavy. To cut down, research thoroughly in advance, and photocopy on both sides of the paper those pages you need for your itinerary. You can enlarge or reduce them, cut off the margins, and staple sheets together. Organize them in labeled manila envelopes: for example, Italy, France, and so on. After you use them, give them away to other travelers, fill the empty envelopes with brochures and other memorabilia that you have collected, and mail those home periodically.

Carrying Film

If you haven't gone digital, here are suggestions for film photography. Remove film canisters from their boxes, remove the film from the plastic canisters, and store them in plastic baggies by type of film. Label each roll with a stick-on dot and give it a number (don't cover the barcode). Take a small notebook and record the numbers, then list the shots you take. You will know what's on each roll when you get home, plus you will have a trip diary! Placing a rubber band around the front of the notebook will keep your place and prevent pages from flapping around in the wind.

Buy your film in the United States, as it is very expensive abroad. You can buy prepaid processing mailers from companies such as Shutterfly and PhotoWorks; these allow you to mail off your rolls as you go. They'll be there when you get home!

For film inspection at the airport, place your film in plastic resealable bags and always ask (politely) for hand inspection to avoid the X-ray machine. Kodak recommends that you do not use commercially available lead-lined bags. They are an invitation to have the X-ray machine turned up. If your camera has film in it, always ask for that, too, to be inspected by hand.

Keep all cameras and camcorders loaded with batteries and able to function upon request during inspections. Cameras that do not function can be viewed as a security risk, leading to delays in passing customs.

Digital

It makes good sense to go digital on your trip. Even if you want to carry a film camera, consider adding a digital camera to your packing list. First, digital media poses no problem when you go through security. X-ray machines at security screening will not damage your digital media (although you should never pack a camera or digital storage media in your checked luggage). Digital media and cell-phone cameras make it easy for you to send pictures home and print out pictures on the road. You can quickly make backups on CD or other media as you travel.

Digitals are light and, in some cases, can spare you the hassle of carrying a heavy flash. Just be sure to bring along plenty of extra batteries and a manual. If you're new to digital photography, be sure to take a class or gain some experience with your camera before hitting the road. You want to understand your camera and make sure it understands you before reaching your destination. Not sure which model to buy? I recommend visiting a good camera store where experienced staff can answer all your questions and arrange for repairs. And if you're considering video, there are now one-time-use video cameras with a small playback screen available at CVS Pharmacies for around $30. They record up to twenty minutes of video. Processing onto DVD costs $12.99. Unfortunately, you cannot plug it into a TV.

The following list will help you equip yourself for most sightseeing ventures:

☐ guidebooks (pages reduced when photocopied) in envelopes, or pages torn out of books

☐ language phrasebook or visual translator

☐ map, general (pick up local ones on the road)

☐ magnifier (flat plastic type) or combo flashlight-magnifier

☐ small spiral notebook or travel journal

☐ compass

☐ pens or colored pencils and a small lightweight sketchbook if you're artistic, or other compact art supplies

☐ clips to keep papers together

☐ camera, flash, plenty of film, batteries (or digital smart cards, batteries, cable)

☐ video camera, tapes, recharger

☐ small binoculars or opera glasses

Extras might include

☐ filters, lenses

☐ a travel mini tripod

☐ dustproof or watertight bag to protect equipment

☐ film cooler with synthetic ice for hot climates

- [ ] prepaid film-processing mailing envelopes
- [ ] folding seat
- [ ] swim goggles
- [ ] other _____

Miscellaneous Gear

The following lists will help you organize various other aspects of your trip.

Eating and Drinking

You may want to bring the following if you will be picnicking or taking care of some of your own meals and you're unsure of what kitchen equipment will be available to you.

A pocketknife is very useful; however, they are not allowed in carry-on luggage. If you do not want to check your bag, plan on buying the knife abroad. They come fitted with a variety of tools. Choose the smallest one that has what you really need: a knife, a bottle opener, a can opener, and a corkscrew. Other tools, such as sawtooth blades, scissors, and magnifiers, are also useful.

You can pack a *blunt* plastic or metal cutlery knife.

Orikaso makes an extremely lightweight and durable dish, bowl, and cup that fold absolutely flat. These are available at REI and Protravel.com.

The weight of a travel coffee maker makes it worthwhile only for brewed-coffee diehards. If you are going abroad, make sure the coffee maker is a dual-voltage appliance or that you have a converter and the right adapters.

- [ ] flask or water bottle
- [ ] water purification method, if needed
- [ ] food or snacks (dried fruit, dried soup, energy bars)
- [ ] pocketknife (see above)

- [ ] bottle, jar, can opener, corkscrew (if not on your pocketknife)
- [ ] spoon (you can eat almost anything with a spoon and a pocket-knife)

For more extensive use, make a portable picnic kit:

- [ ] hot/cold cup
- [ ] utensil set (plastic plate, fork, blunt knife, spoon)
- [ ] beverage coil heater (dual voltage for foreign travel)
- [ ] small cutting board (or cut up those disposable ones)
- [ ] travel towel or antibacterial moist towelettes
- [ ] multipurpose travel soap
- [ ] insulated cooler bag (foldable)
- [ ] tablecloth or large bandanna
- [ ] packets of tea, coffee, sweetener
- [ ] salt, pepper, spices, condiments
- [ ] extra cork or bottle stopper
- [ ] travel coffee maker
- [ ] other _____

Shopping

You can use your regular pocket calculator for currency exchange, but Money Exchange Calculators make handling financial and numerical transactions a breeze. In addition to calculating currency exchanges, they will convert centimeters into inches, kilometers into miles, and Celsius into Fahrenheit. For information on shopping and shipping, see chapter 12.

- [ ] string bag, or use your expandable tote bag or daypack
- [ ] pocket calculator or currency-exchange calculator
- [ ] tape measure

- ☐ magnifying glass (for inspecting jewelry, art, and so on)
- ☐ gift list (with sizes of friends and family members)
- ☐ mailing supplies: duct tape, bubble wrap, blunt scissors
- ☐ other _____

Conversation Starters for Foreign Travel

These may be the most important items in your suitcase. They will help you connect with local people.

- ☐ pictures of your home and family (in plastic cover)
- ☐ language phrasebooks, dictionaries, electronic language translator
- ☐ small gifts and postcards from your state and country
- ☐ other _____

Office Supplies

Remove all packaging and store your supplies in a nylon pouch or zip-locking bag. You may be able to find a small portable office kit that includes many of the items listed here.

- ☐ addresses, home and email (you can preprint on labels and send)
- ☐ spiral notebook, pens, highlighter, permanent marker
- ☐ business cards
- ☐ postcards; extra writing paper, envelopes (I like "fold and mail" stationery—it needs no envelopes!)
- ☐ plastic baggies
- ☐ Scotch or duct tape
- ☐ sticky notes

- [ ] rubber bands
- [ ] paper clips
- [ ] vinyl-coated spring clips (these multipurpose clips can hold papers or can be used to hang clothes from a clothesline), available at art and education supply stores and websites
- [ ] small stapler, staples
- [ ] 10 x 13-inch mailing envelopes
- [ ] shipping supplies
- [ ] other _____

Mobile Computing

For more information on current mobile-computing needs, log on to www.teleadapt.com, www.walkabouttravelgear.com, or www.warrior.com. You can buy many types of special kits and bags that accommodate and protect small electronic equipment and accessories. For more information, see Traveling with a Laptop Computer, page 152.

Current Techno Gear

- [ ] laptop computer, accessories
- [ ] component case
- [ ] PDA and accessories
- [ ] cellular phone, charger
- [ ] MP3 player/iPod
- [ ] adapter for airline power source
- [ ] cable lock to prevent laptop theft
- [ ] modem telecoupler and foreign phone-jack adapters or other connectivity equipment
- [ ] USB memory stick

- ☐ battery chargers or multiple charger, such as iGo
- ☐ batteries
- ☐ converter, adapter
- ☐ foreign surge protector
- ☐ screen-cleaning pads
- ☐ computer tool kit
- ☐ telephone calling card
- ☐ other _____

World Guide to Voltages and Outlet Types

Many countries require more than one type of plug. Below are the most commonly found types. For a description of the letter codes, see pp. 81–82.

Afghanistan—B/D/F
Albania—B/D
Algeria*—B/D/F
American Samoa*—
   A/D/E
Angola—B/D
Antigua—A/C
Argentina—D/E
Armenia—B/D/E
Australia—E
Austria—B/D
Azores—B/D/F
Bahamas*—A
Bahrain—C
Bangladesh—B/D/F
Barbados*—A
Belgium—B

Belize*—A/C
Bermuda*—A
Bhutan—B/D/F
Bolivia*—A/D
Bosnia-Herzegovina—D
Botswana—C/F
Brazil*—A/D
Brunei—C
Bulgaria—D
Burma (Myanmar)—
   B/C/D
Burundi—D
Cambodia—A/D/C
Cameroon*—D
Canada*—A
Canary Islands—D
Cayman Islands*—A

Central African Rep.—D
Chad—B/D/F
Chile—D
China—A/C/D/E
CIS (former USSR)—D
Colombia*—A
Congo—D
Cook Islands—E
Costa Rica*—A/C
Croatia—D
Cuba*—A/D
Cyprus—C/D
Czechoslovakia—D
Denmark—D
Dominica—A/D/E/F
Dominican Rep.*—A
Ecuador*—A/D

*110 volts or a combination of 110 volts and 220 volts; all others, 220 volt
† denotes plug unique to country

Egypt—D	Japan*—A	Netherlands—B
El Salvador*—A	Jordan—C/D/F	Neth. Antilles*—A/B
England—C/D	Kampuchea—D	New Caledonia—B
Equatorial Guinea—D	Kazakhstan—B	New Hebrides—E
Estonia—B/D	Kenya—B/C	New Zealand—E
Ethiopia—D/F	Korea (N and S)—A/B	Nicaragua*—A
Fiji—E	Kuwait—C/D	Niger—A/D/F
Finland—D/D	Laos A/D	Nigeria—C/D/F
France—B/D	Latvia—B	Norway—B
French Guiana—D/F	Lebanon*—B	Oman—C
French Polynesia*—A/D	Lesotho—C/D/F	Pakistan—B/D
Gabon—D	Liberia*—A/C/F	Panama*—A
Gambia—B/C	Libya*—A/C/D/F	Papua New Guinea—E
Germany—B	Liechtenstein—D	Paraguay—D
Ghana—C/D/F	Lithuania—D	Peru*—A/D
Gibraltar—C/D	Luxembourg—D	Philippines*—A/D
Greece—B/D/F	Macao—C/D/F	Poland—D
Greenland—D	Macedonia—B/D	Portugal—C/D
Grenada—C/D/F	Madagascar*—D	Puerto Rico*—A
Guadeloupe—B/D	Malawi—C	Qatar—C
Guam*—A	Malaysia—C	Romania—B
Guatemala*—A	Maldives—A/C/D/F	Russia—B
Guinea—B/D	Mali—D	Rwanda—D
Guyana*—A/D/F	Malta—C	St. Kitts-Nevis—A/C/F
Haiti*—A	Martinique—D	St. Lucia—C
Honduras*—A	Mauritania—D	St. Maarten*—D
Hong Kong—C	Mauritius—C/D	St. Vincent—A/C*/D/E/F
Hungary—B	Mexico*—A	Saudi Arabia*—A/C/D
Iceland—B	Micronesia*—A	Scotland—C
India—D/F	Moldova—B	Senegal*—D/C
Indonesia*—B	Monaco—B	Serbia-Montenegro—B
Iran—D	Mongolia—D	Seychelles—C/F
Iraq—C/D/F	Morocco*—D	Sierra Leone—C/F
Ireland—C/D	Mozambique—D/F	Singapore—A/C
Israel—D/E	Myanmar(formerly	Slovakia—B/D
Italy—D	Burma)—C/D/E/F	Slovenia—B
Ivory Coast—B/D	Namibia—C/F	Solomon Islands—E
Jamaica*—A	Nepal—D/F	Somalia—D

* 110 volts or a combination of 110 volts and 220 volts; all others, 220 volts
† denotes plug unique to country

South Africa, Rep. of†—F	Thailand—A/D	USSR (former)—D
Spain—D	Togo*—D	Uzbekistan—B/E
Sri Lanka—F	Tonga*—A/E	Venezuela*—A
Sudan—C/D/F	Trinidad/Tobago*—A/C/F	Vietnam*—A/D
Surinam*—A/D	Tunisia—D	Virgin Is. (Amer.)*—A
Swaziland—F	Turkey—D	Virgin Is. (Brit.)—B/C
Sweden—D	Turkmenistan—A/B	Wales—C
Switzerland—D	Uganda—C/F	Western Samoa—E
Syria—D	Ukraine—B	Yemen—A/B/C/D
Tahiti—A	United Arab Emir.—C	Yugoslavia (former)—B
Taiwan*—A	United Kingdom—C	Zaire—D/F
Tajikistan—B	United States*—A	Zambia—C/D/F
Tanzania—C/F	Uruguay—B/E	Zimbabwe—C/F

110 volts or a combination of 110 volts and 220 volts; all others, 220 volt
† denotes plug unique to country

Electrical Appliances

Traveling with electrical appliances can be a nuisance because they are heavy and bulky. Do you really need that hairdryer or iron? If you do, pack the smallest, lightest model you can find (dual voltage for foreign travel), with the right adapter plug(s) if you will be out of the country.

Choosing the right electrical configuration for your appliance can be complex. To be able to use the appliance for foreign travel, you will need an adapter plug because outlets abroad are all different. If your appliance is not dual voltage you may also need a voltage converter or transformer. Consult a specialty travel store, luggage store, or merchant specializing in electrical merchandise who is familiar with foreign travel and the equipment you might need. What follows is a guide to familiarize yourself with the subject.

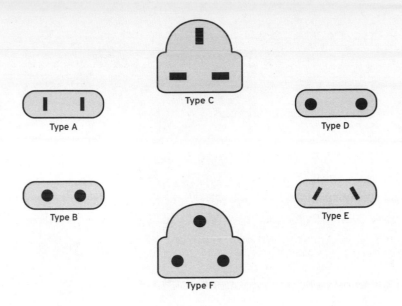

Type C

Type A

Type D

Type B

Type E

Type F

Adapter Plugs

You need adapter plugs for foreign travel for all appliances because wall outlets are different in different places. In some countries you will find more than one type of wall socket in the same room! Slip the appropriate adapter onto the plug of your dual voltage appliance or onto your converter or transformer, then plug it into the wall.

Adapter plugs such as those illustrated above are the most common types. However, other variations do exist, including three-pronged plugs, with or without a grounding pin.

Check the illustrations above and the World Guide to Voltages and Outlet Types on pages 78–80 and purchase the right adapter plug(s) for the wall sockets you may encounter. The illustrations correspond to the following adapters for the most commonly found outlets. Please note that they may be named differently by different vendors.

- Type A—Flat, parallel blades
- Type B—Fat, round pins

- Type C—Three rectangular prongs
- Type D—Thin, round pins (use this plug for recessed outlets)
- Type E—Flat, angled blades
- Type F—Three round holes

Adapter Plugs with Grounding Pins

Adapter plugs with a ground (which minimizes risk of electric shock) are available (see appendix 2, Resources). They slip onto the three-pronged, grounded American plug. There are eleven different grounding plugs for different countries.

Converters and Transformers

A converter or transformer allows your 110 volt (single-voltage) U.S. appliance to run on the 220- or 240-volt current found in many foreign countries. (Some countries, such as Japan and Mexico, run on 110 volts, as we do.) Others may use both 110 volts and 220 volts! *If you have dual-voltage appliances, you do not need a converter. All you need to do is buy the adapter plug(s) and adjust the voltage on the appliance.*

Most converters and low-wattage transformers are designed for intermittent use. Using them continuously may cause the appliance to wear out quickly. Because American appliances are run on 60 cycles and foreign appliances on 50 cycles, your appliance may not work as fast, even with a transformer. Hairdryers should be set on low to avoid overheating. Some models have safety locks that disable the high speed when they are used on 220 or 240 volts.

Transformers for sustained use, as with computers, modems, printers, sewing machines, cassette players, and so on, are available. See pages 84–85 for the section on heavy-duty transformers.

Single Voltage Appliances

If you have a single-voltage appliance, read below to determine what kind of converter or transformer you need. There are two types of converters: high-wattage and low-wattage. The one you need depends on how many watts your appliance uses and what type of appliance you have. Note that converters for these two types of appliances are not interchangeable.

High-Wattage Converters (between 50 and 1600 Watts)
These are required for heat-producing appliances such as hairdryers, irons, steamers, food or bottle warmers, travel coffee makers, curling irons, and heating coils for beverages.

Low-Wattage Converters (up to 50 Watts)
These are for electronic or motorized appliances such as battery rechargers, shavers, contact lens sterilizers, electric toothbrushes, strobes, flashes, massagers, radios, calculators, tape recorders and cassette players, sound conditioners (white noise machines), and video camcorders. Converters for electronic or *motorized* appliances are also called transformers.

Combination High/Low Converter
These are multipurpose and accommodate both high- and low-wattage appliances.

To Select a Converter
1. Determine whether yours is a heat-producing appliance or a motorized, electronic appliance.

2. Determine the wattage consumption and cycle ratings. These are usually indicated on the item. Always check the actual wattage consumption of the unit to get the proper size of transformer.

Other Gadgets You May Need

Battery Eliminator

This device will let you plug your battery-operated appliance, such as a personal tape player, cassette player, or radio (if it has a DC jack), into the wall instead of consuming an endless amount of batteries.

A "Reverse" Transformer

This device enables you to use a foreign 220- or 240-volt motorized, electronic appliance (up to 50 watts) on North American 110-volt current. These transformers are useful for visitors to our country and for those things you picked up while traveling. These will not work on heat-producing appliances, such as hairdryers.

A Heavy-Duty Transformer

If your equipment's wattage consumption exceeds the ratings of the small converters, you will need heavy-duty transformers. These are also necessary for continuous use (more than thirty minutes at a time), such as for small and large computers, modems, and printers, regardless of wattage consumption listed on the appliance.

Always check the exact consumption to select the right transformer. A good rule of thumb is to double the level. For example, if your appliance is 100 watts, choose a transformer that is 200 watts. Transformers come in 200-, 300-, 500-, 750-, and 1,000-watt sizes and are available in electrical shops, from specialty relocation merchants, and in well-stocked travel stores (see appendix 2, Resources). Powerful transformers are large and very heavy. Think twice before taking one along.

Motorized, electronic appliances that require large transformers include computers, printers, modems, and photocopiers, as well as large radios, stereos, tape decks, large and small food mixers, food processors, blenders, sewing machines, refrigerators, power drills, large medical devices, and typewriters. Many small computers and laptop and notebook computers come in dual-voltage models. If they are not dual voltage, check the wattage for the right size of transformer, but keep in mind that for use from over thirty minutes to an hour, a heavy-duty transformer is recommended. Fax machines do not work reliably even with a transformer. Heat-producing appliances that may require larger transformers include electric blankets, large coffee makers, percolators, and large hotplates.

Lamps

North American lamps will run in Europe with a 100-watt converter (and adapter plug). However, bring extra 100-watt or lower bulbs because you won't find them easily abroad. It may be easier to either buy a desk lamp overseas or purchase a battery-operated reading light. Some models have an optional dual-voltage transformer that can be connected to the lamp and plugged into an outlet with the appropriate adapter plug, to cut down on battery consumption. If you plan to use this to read in bed, an extension cord may be handy to pack.

4

THE CARRY-ON
WARDROBE

I used to ask my audiences what they thought a travel wardrobe was, and I would get some uncertain looks! Yes, we know it has to fit in our suitcase. And ideally we won't have to iron. And of course we'd like to look nice and feel good about what we're wearing. But what else?

Your travel wardrobe is hardworking. It must do many things for you. First and foremost, it must function to protect you from the elements. Whether you expect heat, humidity, wind, or rain, these few pieces of clothing must keep you either (1) cool and ventilated or (2) warm and dry. And sometimes they must do both!

Second, travel clothing must be versatile. With only a few items in your suitcase, you must be prepared for almost any type of occasion—rural day hike, cosmopolitan city tour, nice restaurant, or theatre, possibly all in the same day. So your clothes should provide you with lots of outfits, created from a few basic mix-and-match items. Each item, carefully considered for style, serves a purpose. Simple styles will take you a long way!

Third, your wardrobe must be maintainable. Whether you are washing in the sink, making a weekly trip to the laundromat, or sending out your laundry at your hotel, the clothes you bring should fit your particular washing plans. This may change from trip to trip.

So, if you want to go carry-on instead of hauling lots of bags, you have to choose your wardrobe carefully. Your limited number of garments must serve you in a wide variety of social and climatic situations. Functionality, versatility, and maintainability are your primary considerations. Each of these may have a different priority depending on the type of trip and weather you expect.

The more time you take to refine your wardrobe, the better it will serve you!

How Much to Take

Trips vary in length, climate, and activities, and in how mobile and self-sufficient you want to be. Sometimes you want to travel ultralight; other times you need more clothing choices and don't care as much about the number of bags you carry. I have divided wardrobe plans into three approaches and one hybrid. For each trip, pick a packing approach that matches your activities, climate, and mobility and self-sufficiency levels.

The Minimalist Approach

The minimalist travels very light. The wash-and-wear wardrobe is perfect for temperate weather, for short trips (between two and five days), and for single-purpose trips that are entirely casual or entirely business. You will be washing often and wearing the same outfits frequently. With no more than 20 pounds, you will experience incredible mobility; you will easily be able to carry all of your luggage on any kind of public transportation.

The Moderate Approach

Most carry-on travelers will take the moderate approach. A basic travel wardrobe of eight to ten pieces will prepare you for temperature swings and varying activities. Your laundry schedule will be somewhat relaxed. You will have several choices for day and evening, an advantage if you will be with the same people continually and would like some variety in your wardrobe. The moderate wardrobe is the most that many people can fit comfortably in a 22-inch carry-on.

The Luxury Approach

For those who prefer to have available as many options in clothing and accessories as possible, the luxury approach is the one to choose. You may be going to formal or business events that require certain types of clothing. You may need to prepare for very cold weather or special activities. The extra convenience may justify a heavier carry-on, larger suitcase, or addition of a second bag. And be prepared: you may have to check your luggage. Either way, you've lost a little of your mobility.

The Multipurpose Approach

Assume that your trip requires two distinct wardrobes: one for cold weather and one for warm, or one for business and one for casual. How do you pack for two purposes in a single carry-on? The answer is to pack two minimalist wardrobes (or one minimalist and one moderate), one for each segment of your trip. The three-compartment carry-on is the best bag for such trips. Pack two wardrobes, each in its own compartment, and use the third compartment for toiletries (see chapter 6 for packing instructions).

Clothing Guidelines

Whatever the purpose of the trip, you can assemble a good travel wardrobe by keeping a few guidelines in mind:

- Take only comfortable clothes, choosing garments that will accommodate a security wallet.

- Select versatile garments in simple styles.

- Select compact, easily maintained fabrics. Take advantage of the new breed of wrinkle-resistant, quick-dry materials.

- Pack separates.

- Choose a color scheme and stick to it.

- Pack thin clothing that can be layered, rather than bulky garments.

- Try to blend in and respect local customs.

Meet all these conditions and your clothes will easily fit into a carry-on bag!

Such clothes do exist, and finding them is a matter of thinking about the requirements and making good choices: simple styles are more likely to be appropriate and lack bulk, separates are versatile and comfortable, comfortable clothing is likely to be easily maintained and offer room for a security wallet, and a color scheme and separates will make your wardrobe choices expand exponentially. This is what this chapter is all about. In it, we will consider the guidelines and the various garments that you will be taking.

Comfort

We often give up comfort for fashion's sake. Don't! Choose loose-fitting garments and cushioned, broken-in shoes. Loose-fitting clothes will accommodate under-garment security wallets.

For extended plane, car, and bus travel, wear comfortable, roomy garments that breathe, such as knits. Loose-fitting skirts or pants with elasticized or drawstring waistbands and shoes that leave room for expanded feet are essential. Take a pair of soft folding slippers, flip-flops, or thick socks to wear during the flight.

Even if you are a minimalist, you can add a "travel day" outfit to the wardrobe list: a skirt or comfortable pair of pants and a shirt, or a nice knit warm-up outfit. You can also wear your principal jacket, skirt or pants, and blouse or shirt. Your sweater can remain in your main bag or day bag.

If you are a moderate or luxury traveler, choose any garment combination you plan to take. Wear the heaviest items to reduce your packing load. If you are traveling from a cold climate to a hot one, dress for arrival, not departure. Do not arrive in Hawaii at Christmas in your overcoat!

The Color Scheme

Start with a color scheme. Space is too valuable to be wasted on odd pieces of clothing that cannot be combined with other items. The practical travel wardrobe consists of separates revolving around one basic, neutral color scheme. This allows you to mix and match items freely to create different looks. Chico's recommends the "2 + 1" formula: wear any two items of the same color and add one more in a contrasting material or color.

Think about it—that's a lot of different outfits!

Use a shirt or blouse, scarf, ties, belt, and other accessories to add one or two accent colors. Choosing a color scheme also limits the number of pairs of shoes you have to bring. Limiting yourself to one color combination gives you a framework for shopping. Color can make you feel good and look good and create appropriate impressions in all kinds of situations. Items that do not fit in the color scheme simply do not go!

Before you try to decide on particular colors, look over your clothes. Do you see a color pattern that you prefer? Do you have enough items for any one color to form the basis for a wardrobe? Research the customs of the countries you plan to visit. In some countries, it is inappropriate for tourists to wear certain colors that have a particular cultural significance.

Choose lighter colors for warm weather and medium and darker colors for cooler climates and because they show the dirt less. Darker colors are safe and versatile in any situation. These colors are also more versatile because they are appropriate for day or evening. Choose neutral tones for the basic pieces of your wardrobe and for warm weather travel. Choose solids rather than prints, except for a two-piece dress and perhaps a blouse. Solids mix and match easily and can be conveniently transformed from day to evening, from casual to fancy. For shirts, blouses, sweaters, and accessories, you can choose from a wider variety of accent colors.

The following are neutral, seasonless colors:

- Blacks—all shades
- Gray—silvery-gray, light and medium gray, charcoal gray, and all in between
- Neutral beiges—beige, camel, taupe, tan, khaki, cream, ivory, sand
- Brown—cocoa, rust, chocolate, smoke brown, and others
- Navy—nautical, bright, black navy, royal

If you like to wear a little more color, consider these:

- Bright neutrals—red, teal, purple, jade
- Deep neutrals—forest green, hunter green, deep teal, burgundy, rust, copper, plum, cocoa, tan, taupe, khaki, sage

These colors can be used as accents, too. The following neutrals work on their own only in spring and summer but may be worn as accents all year long:

- Pastels, light and dark—pink, yellow, mint green, lavender, peach
- White—seasonless in shirts and blouses only; in other pieces, such as jackets, dresses, slacks, and so on, it is for summer only

The charts on page 92 show color combinations derived from neutral schemes. Once you have chosen the basic wardrobe pieces and shoes, add other blouses, shirts, shoes, and accessories in coordinating accent colors.

Wardrobe Color Planner—Women

First neutral color (for jackets, skirts and slacks)	Beige	Navy	Black	Bright	Gray
Second neutral color (for shirts, blouses and sweaters)	navy white or ivory black *casual only:* pastels bright neutrals deep neutrals	neutral beiges white or ivory burgundy gray *casual only:* bright neutrals deep neutrals	white or ivory khaki taupe gray neutral beiges	black white or ivory gray navy neutral beiges	white or ivory black camel navy *casual only:* pink peach yellow
Shoes, belts, and handbags	neutral brown	navy	black gray	black	gray black neutral
Accent colors (for accessories, blouses, jewelry)	earth tones gold ivory bright colors deep colors	red burgundy gold silver bright colors	red gold white ivory silver	silver gold white ivory bright colors	red burgundy deep green pastels silver gold

Wardrobe Color Planner—Men

First neutral color (for suits, jackets, and slacks)	Beige/brown	Navy	Black	Gray
Second neutral color (for shirt and second pair of slacks)	white or ivory brown any other beige	neutral beige white or ivory burgundy gray	gray white or ivory	black navy burgundy
Shoes and belts	brown	black	black	black
Accent colors	earth tones burgundy or red pastels brights deeps	gold red hunter green	red	burgundy red

Fabrics

We overpackers are fortunate to live in an era of space-age synthetic fabrics. It is amazing how many of them are comfortable, wrinkle-resistant, fast-drying, attractive, and functional to boot! Take advantage of these fabrics and incorporate them into your wardrobe. Many of them can be found in outdoor and travel stores, in catalogs, or online.

For nice casual wear, you can find cotton or cotton/polyester pants and shirts with a wrinkle-resistant finish. If it's important that your clothes dry quickly, consider the various performance fabrics such as Supplex nylon, NANO-TEX (treated cotton), and specific synthetic blends. There is even insect-repellent clothing!

As far as natural fabrics go, cotton, cotton/polyester, and linen are still preferred choices for summer heat. Just embrace the wrinkles or be prepared for them. Relaxed, open, or mesh weaves are easier to care for and cooler than tightly woven fabrics.

For winter cold and for business, choose wool. A year-round weight (9 ounces) will keep you cool when it is hot and warm when it is cold. Or pack merino knits—comfortable to sleep in! And wool is packing-resilient—its fibers recover when you hang it up.

The chart on page 94 lists recommended travel fabrics. For more details, see Protection from the Elements: Layering, on page 100.

Sun-Protective Fabrics

Some fabrics reflect or absorb the sun's UV rays, providing some protection for your skin. Conventional fabrics include unbleached cottons, high-luster polyesters, thin satiny silk, darker colors, and tightly-woven fabrics like denim and cotton duck (*San Jose Mercury News*, May 31, 1995). Sun Precautions, Sun Clothing, Etc., and other companies offer clothing and hats that they rate 30+ SPF and above (see appendix 2, Resources).

NOTE: Although clothes can provide real protection, you should use sunscreen for maximum protection, particularly on exposed areas of the body.

Recommended Fabrics for Travel Wardrobes

	Cold-to-mild climates (three seasons)	Warm-to-hot climates
Jackets, skirts, slacks, and shorts *Choose medium- to light-weight fabrics for year-round wear-ability. Wool gabardine and knits are especialy recommended.*	100% wool gabardine wool/synthetic blends 100% polyester (i.e., microfiber) merino wool jersey knits synthetic suede rayon and rayon blends cotton jersey knits, heavier weight viscose blends 100% silk*	lightweight wool gabardine cotton or cotton/polyester knits natural/synthetic blends with linen look viscose and other synthetic blends 100% cotton* cotton/polyester polyester crepe de chine handwashable silk* silk—raw, hopsack, and tweed* Supplex nylon linen* Tencel/cotton
Sweaters/warm shirts *Choose medium to light weight.*	100% wool (angora, cashmere, lambswool, merino, etc.) wool and synthetic blends 100% acrylic cotton/cotton blend knits in heavier weights Polartec fleece/micro fleece wool flannel	100% cotton knits cotton/polyester knits cotton/silk blends cotton/linen blends* cotton chamois or flannel
Skirts/blouses	cotton/synthetic blends polyester crepe de chine rayon and rayon crepe* various synthetic blends silk jacquard and other silks* silk-like synthetics	cotton knits cotton/viscose cotton/synthetic blends polyester crepe de chine various natural/synthetic blends 100% cotton* linen* Tencel/cotton
Dresses and two-piece dresses	wool jersey knits wool and synthetic blend knits wool or rayon challis* washable silk and raw silk* cotton knits, heavy weight various synthetic blends (including viscose acetate, etc.)	cotton and cotton blend knits cotton crepe or gauze cotton/polyester blends rayon crepe* linen/synthetic blends various natural/synthetic blends linen* Tencel/cotton

* Needs ironing or steaming

Insect-Repellent Apparel

BUZZ OFF fabric is specifically made to ward off all types of insects without harsh chemicals. A patented process incorporates the cotton or synthetic fibers with permethrin, a man-made form of a natural insect repellent found in the chrysanthemum plant. For manufacturer's information see www.exofficio.com/buzzoff. Like DEET, it must be used with care—if you have concerns about the toxicity of permethrin and other synthetic pyrethroids, I recommend doing a bit of internet research for the most up-to-date health information.

Separates

Separates allow you to mix and match easily and extend the uses of your wardrobe. They are also easier to pack. Men, of course, have no problem in this department. A sport coat or jacket, sweater or vest, khakis or slacks, shirt and the occasional tie will get you into almost any theater or restaurant.

For women, five pieces can form the base of your wardrobe—a jacket, skirt, slacks, and two blouses can create so many outfits. Instead of packing a dress, think about adding a two-piece dress: a skirt and button-down blouse made of the same fabric in a solid, stripe, or print. This can expand your wardrobe exponentially and pack like a dream. In a knit, washable silk, or rayon crepe, they can be worn for day or evening, for casual or dressy occasions. They can also be mixed and matched with your other items in many combinations. Dresses are bulkier to pack and limit access to your security wallet. If you must take one, choose a very simple, neutral-colored chemise or shirtwaist dress in a fabric that can be worn in the day or evening.

Other excellent choices are the unstructured jacket or blazer with ample room for layering; A-line, straight, wrap-around, or not-too-full skirts (with pockets); split skirts; shirts and blouses in scoop-neck, camp-shirt, turtleneck, button-down, and polo styles; and coordinated knit sweater or jacket sets. All your bottom garments and jackets should have pockets.

If you want to add a little extra drama to your outfits, Chico's women's clothing store suggests pairing two plain garments with one novelty item. For example, a matching shirt and pants in black can be paired with a colorful patterned jacket. Or a neutral jacket and slacks can be worn with a printed or bright shirt. This is a great formula to keep in mind for an interesting and fun wardrobe.

Multifunctional Garments

Stay away from jumpsuits and dresses that are designed for specific functions. Look at every garment and think of the different ways you can wear it: A large T-shirt can replace a robe, beach cover-up, and sleepwear. Long underwear, cotton tights, or yoga pants can be worn in bed. A knit warm-up suit can be slept in or worn down the hall to the bathroom. A skirt and blouse in the same fabric can be a two-piece dress or two separate outfits. A long wool knit cardigan and pants can be nice enough for a restaurant or slept in on a long bus ride. A simple button-down camp shirt can be casual or dressy. Polo shirts are more versatile than conventional T-shirts and protect your neck from the sun as well. Walking shorts can double as swim trunks. A sweater with gold buttons can be casual or dressy. If it has a V-neck and no pockets, it can also be worn backwards.

Simple Styles

Simplicity will get you by in any situation, casual or dressy. You can also get years of wear out of your wardrobe if you choose classic styles. Simple styles are also easier to pack; drapey skirts and pleats are more difficult and more time consuming to care for on the road. Also, a classic look guarantees acceptance in most parts of the world, no matter what the custom.

Sleepwear and Loungewear

Nothing feels as comforting after a long day of sightseeing as curling up in your hotel room with a good book. But loungewear and sleepwear consume lots of space. When choosing specific items, keep these tips in mind.

A dress-length T-shirt can be worn as a nightgown and as a swim cover-up, bathrobe, or even a dress (add a nice belt or sash). For insulation, wear long underwear underneath or a turtleneck.

For leg warmth, add silk, cotton, or Coolmax leggings. Athletic leggings can also be worn for exercise. Or pack a pair of black drawstring yoga pants.

Sleep in long underwear. Silk- or polyester-knit shirts and leggings will keep you warm and are cozy to wear. Try a medium weight.

A knit warm-up suit is perfect—light knit training pants and a hoodie sweatshirt. You can sleep in it and go out to get a coffee in it!

If you still want conventional sleepwear, choose a very packable lightweight nightgown, pajamas, and/or a robe.

Maintenance

Choose the type and amount of clothing that you will be able to maintain according to the laundry services available. Are you going to do your own wash? How often? Are there dry cleaners where you are going? Are there laundromats? Take great care in choosing fabrics. Fill out the Itinerary Wardrobe Planner to pin down your laundry opportunities (see p. 118) whether you want to lug an iron or steamer. If you do not, stick to wrinkle-resistant, drip-dry hand washables. Find out about the cost, quality, and availability of dry cleaning before taking lots of dry-clean-only fabrics. Make sure you carry stain-removing supplies with you (see pp. 68–69).

Garment Shields

I think these are a great wardrobe discovery for travel. These are perspiration guards that you slip over your bra and under your shirt or dress. For women, I suggest taking two pairs of removable garment shields. Men can also use removable underarm pads. You can wash one pair and wear one pair, and they'll dry overnight, keeping your shirt perspiration free. They are available online at www.kleinertsshields.com. Kleinerts also makes and sells protective T-shirts with built-in underarm padding for men and women. Garment shields will cut your laundering frequency way down, since you do not have to wash merely because of underarm perspiration.

Formal Wear or Special Events

Even cruises that have one or two formal evenings no longer require evening gowns and tuxedos; in most cases a silky dress and a dark jacket and tie are the norm, especially on large cruise ships. Most of the smaller ships are much less formal. For formal events and evening wear, select elegant packable fabrics such as a silky synthetics, jersey knits in wool or nylon, rayon crepe, and synthetic blends. Use accessories to add flair.

No matter what packing approach you have chosen, dress-up wear will be limited. For the minimalist traveler, the two-piece dress (or a skirt or slacks and dressy blouse or cardigan) with a bright scarf or belt might be as dressy as you get. Moderate and luxury travelers have a bit more choice in the two-piece dress and another dressier outfit. But don't fret! A simple chemise can be dressed up with a scarf and necklace. Pants and a blouse, or a two-piece dress in a silky-feeling polyester microfiber will be very lightweight and compact (see Tilley Endurables in appendix 2, Resources). A black rayon crepe skirt or wide palazzo-style pants with blouse make compact evening wear.

Respect Local Customs

Research the areas you are going to visit. Consult your travel agent, guidebooks, and experienced travelers to find out about the standards of acceptable dress. In many foreign countries, modesty is the norm. Clothing should not be revealing in any way. Women should bring a scarf to cover the head and shoulders at religious sites. Avoid wearing shorts and low-cut blouses, skirts above the knee, and swimwear when you are away from the beach. If you must bring shorts, choose a baggy, knee-length style.

The climate of your destination can dictate your choice of color. Sunny places and informal cultures call for light, bright colors. In the large, older metropolitan areas of Europe and South America, tailored clothes in neutral and dark colors are more the norm. The color black is accepted as modern and sophisticated all year long in many large metropolitan cities in Europe, South America, and the United States. It may, however, look too somber in sunny Asian cities, the Mediterranean, and other coastal resort areas. Bright colors are acceptable there.

Clothing styles vary from city to city, even in the United States. Some countries require more formal dress; others are less restrictive. For example, in European cities, slacks are generally not worn by women to work or in dressy restaurants. Suit jackets are worn in offices and restaurants and on the street. In India, a conservative suit would be inappropriate for a woman among the bright-colored saris. The safest strategy is to be tastefully dressed, perhaps on the conservative side. This means a jacket and tie (or a dark sweater and tie) for men and a skirt and blouse or shirtwaist dress for women. For casual occasions, a button-down or polo-style shirt with short or long sleeves will always look appropriate. You can buy garments of the local style in the country you are visiting. In many countries, casual clothes such as jeans, jogging suits, athletic shoes, T-shirts, shorts, and resort wear will mark you as a tourist and should be reserved for the outdoors and resort areas.

In the Middle East and Asia, shoes are often removed in homes, temples, and mosques. Take shoes that are easy to put on and take off. (For visiting temples, tennis socks can be tucked into your day bag.) Observe your host and those around you to determine whether shoes are appropriate.

Bikinis are not acceptable at many destinations, and in others are worn only by tourists. In resort areas that attract an international clientele, they are the norm. Ask your travel agent for advice and travel with a conservative one-piece suit unless you are sure a bikini is appropriate.

Try to avoid the "tourist" look that can make you a target for unsavory types with nimble hands. Nylon jogging suits, white athletic shoes, loud patterns, and bright colors are a giveaway.

(Of course, loud behavior does nothing to improve the image.)

Protection from the Elements: Layering

Layering means wearing several complementary lightweight garments rather than one or two bulky ones. Because different fabrics and fibers have different qualities, the layering pieces must be made in appropriate fibers, weights, and fabrics so that warmth, ventilation, and wind and moisture resistance will be provided without hindering your mobility.

The best approach is to pack thin layers of clothing that can be added or peeled off as the temperature changes. Avoid packing bulky sweaters and coats unless they are absolutely necessary. If you need heavy items for only part of your trip, consider sending them home after you are finished using them. You can also use compression bags to pack bulky items (see chapter 6, How to Pack Your Suitcase). But try not to depend on these—if they malfunction you're stuck!

The concept of layering is so important that I have organized all my travel wardrobes around it.

There are four basic elements to the layering system: an underlayer, a midlayer, an outer layer, and clothing for the extremities.

Layer 1: Underlayer

The underlayer is worn against the skin and has two important functions. The first is to allow excess body heat to be released. The second is to carry (wick) perspiration away from the body. In warm weather, fabric should absorb moisture (as cotton does) or wick it away, keeping the body dry (as Coolmax does). In cold weather, moisture should be transferred (wicked) away from the skin to the outer layers of the clothing, where it evaporates. Thus the body is kept warm and dry, even in wet weather. Moisture should be avoided at all costs, since it makes you miserable and uncomfortable.

Warm-Weather Underlayers

In hot weather, knit T-shirts and tank tops are the perfect foundation for a layering system. In warm weather it might be your only layer. Cotton knit is comfortable, absorbs perspiration, and has a quick-cooling effect. However, in anything but hot and dry weather, it will get wet and stay wet. If you want to pack less and need fast-drying fabric, choose cotton/polyester or other synthetic knits, or "hydrophobic" polyester knit T-shirts and tank tops made with Coolmax and other technical fabrics. These are highly packable and fast-drying, and they add a lot of versatility and performance to your wardrobe. Minimalists may only need two (wash one and wear one).

Choose a variety of styles to be dressed up or down. Polo-type shirts work well for men in a variety of situations, and the collar protects the neck from the sun. For women, polos and simple crewneck styles, wide shoulder straps on tank tops, and appropriate necklines will add comfort and versatility to your wardrobe. Camisoles are a popular alternative, if they will be appropriate.

If temperatures will be cooler at night or at high altitudes, bring a pair of lightweight silk or Coolmax leggings to wear under slacks. These worn under a long T-shirt can also be loungewear and sleepwear too.

Coolmax underwear (briefs, bras, and socks) made of Patagonia's Capilene fiber are perfect for light travelers. Invest in three pairs; they will dry in two to four hours. They will also keep you comfortable and dry. Otherwise, underpants should be of nylon or lightweight cotton in the smallest style you can wear. Another option is Onederwear disposable cotton underwear, which comes in packages of five (see appendix 2, Resources).

Cold-Weather Underlayers

Packable, fast-drying, and hand-washable long underwear is one of the single most important investments you can make if you expect cold weather. It will keep you warm and dry on the coldest rainy nights and keep the chill off during a brisk fall day so you don't need that bulky coat. In fact, it can prepare you for temperature changes of up to 50 degrees. And as an added plus, it doubles as sleepwear—pack two pairs, and you don't have to pack pajamas. Used widely for outdoor activity, modified polyester knits wick moisture away to the outer layers faster than natural fibers will. Polyester readily repels water, remains relatively warm when wet, and dries quickly. The new treated polyester knits, such as Capilene (Patagonia), Moisture Transfer System (MTS, made by REI), Coolmax, Wickers, and Thermax, all have insulating properties. Merino wool is also still in use. These are all machine washable and dryable and do not retain odors. Undershirts and pants, shorts, hats, socks, and gloves are all made from these comfortable materials. Keep in mind that underlayers needn't look like long johns. Look for technical T-shirt and tank-top styles—these can double as long underwear. Coolmax underwear, bras, and T-shirts will wash and dry overnight, so you can take two or three, and that's all you need.

Silk long underwear also provides lightweight, bulkless warmth. It is most suitable as a comfortable layer beneath street clothes. It is also great as sleepwear. The strong silk fibers retain body heat, and the fabric can breathe. Available for men and women in all styles of shirts, camisoles, long underwear, briefs, and turtlenecks— silk underwear is hand washable and drip-dries quickly.

Silk underwear is available throughout the year from the mail-order company Wintersilks. Polyester-knit underwear is available year-round from mail-order catalogs, such as REI, Patagonia, and TravelSmith, and in outdoor stores. Seasonally it is also available from L.L.Bean and Lands' End.

Use lightweight fabrics for highly aerobic activity, medium for stop-and-go and general travel, and heavy for extremely cold climates. If in doubt, it is best to err on the side of lightness; you can always adjust the outer layers for added warmth. Bring extra underwear for cold-weather destinations, as it will dry more slowly.

Layer 2: Midlayer (Regular Clothing and Sweater)

This layer, in the form of shirts, slacks, sweaters, and blazer-type jackets, is an integral part of the system. It traps air and keeps the body warm, offers protection from sunburn, mosquitoes, and the like, and should also wick moisture toward the outside. The particular garments you choose will depend on the weather.

Warm and Hot Weather

Shirts will be worn alone to ventilate the body or layered over your T-shirt (Layer 1) to keep the chill off or protect you from mosquitoes and the sun. For maximum versatility, take loose-fitting, lightweight, button-down shirts and blouses made from cotton or cotton/polyester woven or knit fabrics. For wet or humid conditions, open-weave cotton or cotton mixed with Supplex nylon feels natural, is wrinkle resistant, and dries quickly. Patagonia, Travel-Smith, Norm Thompson, Tilley Endurables, and L.L.Bean sell clothing that is ideal for casual or dressy situations in warm and tropical weather. Coolmax button-down shirts are also available.

For men's dress shirts, the coarser weaves such as oxford cloth do better when packed in a carry-on. Finely woven cottons wrinkle very easily—forget them. Pack coarser-weave cotton and cotton/polyester blend shirts instead. (Lands' End makes a cotton/polyester dress shirt.) For casual shirts, I recommend a wrinkle-resistant weave, such as chambray, twill, or seersucker, or a garment-washed fabric in a light to medium weight. Do not expect the pressed look unless you plan to bring an iron. Make sure to take at least one lightweight, long-sleeved shirt (and hat) for sun protection.

For warm weather, a thin cotton or cotton-blend knit cardigan or pullover sweater is perfect. For women, cardigans are definitely the most versatile. They go with shorts, skirts, and slacks. If you expect temperatures to drop, take a cotton-flannel or chamois-type shirt, a thin wool sweater, or a lightweight Polarfleece sweater, jacket, or vest. Fleece is just as warm as wool but is lighter and more compact and dries quickly. Polarfleece is available under various brand names from L.L.Bean, REI, Patagonia, and other outdoor catalogs and retailers. It comes in three weights—100 (thinnest), 200 (medium weight), and 300 (extra thick). "Softwear" nylon or polyester jersey cardigan-style jackets are also comfortable for women to wear over a tank or T-shirt. They can be dressy and go with a skirt as well. I have seen this at Nordstrom, Chico's, and Norm Thompson.

Jackets such as sport coats and blazers must be made of breathable, pliable, wrinkle-resistant fabric. Tropical- or medium-weight worsted or gabardine wool or wool blends, cotton and polyester blends, polyester microfiber, some silks, cotton, and linen-look blends are all recommended. Spandex is added to many fabrics now to improve their flexibility and comfort; it makes clothing comfortable even on long plane rides. L.L.Bean, Lands' End, and Orvis also offer excellent sport coats for travel. Their jackets typically come in khaki, navy, olive, and brown and have hidden pockets. Darker colors such as navy will give you maximum versatility for casual and dress wear, especially in cities. Lighter colors will do well in the heat.

The world is increasingly informal, and in many places men can get by without a sport coat. A dark pullover sweater, nice slacks, white shirt, and tie will do just fine. Jackets are, however, appropriate in cities for good restaurants and on cruises for the formal nights. Jackets are often essential if you are doing any kind of business. In many parts of the world, they are necessary unless you are on a casual trip. Ask your travel agent or host for advice. If you do take one, try "the uniform"—navy blazer, gray or tan slacks, white shirt, burgundy sweater, tie. This look is appropriate for any occasion.

Dresses can be very comfortable in very hot weather. If you take a dress, look for a neutral chemise style in a packable fabric. This can be transformed easily for day and evening. TravelSmith and

Norm Thompson offer several of these types of dresses. For warm weather, a cotton shirtwaist dress is useful.

Slacks, skirts, and shorts should be made of cotton, cotton/polyester, a packable synthetic, or lightweight wool. Slacks should be loose fitting for ventilation and should not chafe. Roomy pants and shorts are available in Supplex nylon, which is compact, light, and cool, though extremely casual. An extremely wind-resistant fabric, it dries quickly in hot weather, making it ideal for beach, desert, boat, and other warm-weather vacations. Being compact, it is also a good choice for all sorts of active wear.

NOTE: A pair of black pants is indispensable!

People love denim jeans, and they are worn all over the world. They are sturdy and very forgiving in the soil and stain departments, making them perfect travel garments for parents with small children, for some casual travelers, or for "dress-down" days in general. However, jeans are limited as a travel garment when you don't have room to bring a lot of clothes. They don't transition from day into evening, or from casual to dressy occasions. Also, they are bulky, difficult to hand wash, and slow to dry. Finally, if cotton jeans become wet, they stay wet—and so do you.

Jeans are at their best in moderate temperatures—that is, when it's not too hot, cold, or wet. To be a good travel garment, they should be soft, lightweight, loose fitting, and nonchafing. A washer and dryer should be accessible. Otherwise, stick to casual fabrics such as cotton twill, cotton/polyester, supplex nylon, and linen, or TravelSmith's Tencel denim (available in pants, skirts, vest, and a dress).

Skirts should have pockets and be simply styled (one should be midlength). They should also be loose fitting and allow the use of a security wallet. I also like skorts or culottes, especially for cruises.

Shorts should be knee length with lots of pockets. Supplex nylon shorts will double for swim trunks and casual wear; look for the longer versions. A wraparound sarong or pareo can be used by men and women as a swim cover-up. A multipurpose alternative is a big T-shirt that can be worn in a variety of ways (such as a casual dress). Lands' End makes good T-shirt cover-ups.

Temperate to Cold Weather
In cool to cold weather, choose jackets, slacks, and skirts in light- or medium-weight wool and wool blends, heavier cotton and cotton blends, and polyester microfiber. Wool knits, especially merino wool, are excellent for dresses and women's coordinates. They're comfortable enough to sleep in. Sweaters and cardigans should be made of finely knit wool such as cashmere or merino. Or, for casual and active trips, include a lighter-weight polyester fleece jacket or vest for excellent breathability, warmth, and fast-drying properties. Blouses can be cotton/polyester or silk-like synthetics, including polyester. Men (and women) should take travel-worthy, cotton/polyester, long-sleeved oxfords or pinpoints (available from Lands' End for men and women). Add layering pieces such as a knit turtleneck or jewel neck and long-sleeved shirts of cotton knit, chamois, twill, wool flannel, or 100-weight fleece.

Layer 3: Outerlayer (Outerwear and Raingear)

For the general traveler, this top layer will protect against rain, wind, and moisture while allowing body heat to escape. If you choose to bring your London Fog or similar raincoat, keep in mind that it will have to be worn or carried on your arm. (It will take up a lot of room, in the bag, even with a compression bag). Better to choose a coat that is water-repellent (as opposed to waterproof), breathable, and packable. Your style, destinations, and activities will dictate its form. A full-length microfiber raincoat or a coated nylon taffeta version of this is perfect for city sightseeing and evenings at the theater; a nylon anorak is great for casual travel, beach trips, or warm/cool weather trips. To make these coats water-repellent, you can buy ReviveX Wash-In Water Repellent, a liquid that you add to the wash cycle (www.campmor.com). Or you can spray the garment with a water repellant such as ReviveX or

Scotchgard. Follow care instructions for your garment in all cases. Packing a small umbrella is a must.

For more extreme conditions or for "singing in the rain," you may need to substitute or add a layer that is waterproof and breathable. Avid walkers and hikers will need a rainjacket and rain pants or a waterproof poncho. These garments, usually bulkier than their water-repellent counterparts, are made from highly technical, laminated fabrications (the most famous of which is GORE-TEX) and can be found at outdoor stores by manufacturers such as REI, Sierra Designs, and Patagonia.

I don't recommend plastic unless it is for backup use only. Plastic is bulky, heavy, doesn't breathe, and is difficult to reuse.

Layer 4: The Extremities

You can be pretty miserable if your limbs are cold and wet. Layer 4 provides the necessities to protect your head, hands, and feet. Bring a hat for rain or shine. There are myriad hats on the market. Look for one that is wide-brimmed, packable, breathable, and suitable to your activities. "Baseball" type hats should have a large bill. A dark underside absorbs UV rays. Chin straps or a cinch strap around the head are desirable for windy weather. If you need a hat that floats, look for a closed-cell foam layer in the top. To protect your neck from the hot sun, some models, such as the Supplex nylon Skyline Packhat, feature a hanging fabric drape to cover your neck and ears.

Sun hats are made of cotton, wool, felt, hemp, Supplex nylon, or grass (Panama hats). Supplex nylon hats dry fast and protect you from UV rays, as do Solumbra hats, which are rated 30+ SPF .

Rain-or-shine hats are usually made of cotton duck, wool felt, coated Supplex nylon, or waxed cotton. Among many excellent hat manufacturers are Tilley, Ultimate, Watership Trading Company, and Lights of the Sky, Ltd.

Balaclavas, head guards, and headbands for ear covering should all be considered for cold weather.

To protect your hands from cold and wet, consider modified polyester (such as Capilene) or silk-knit glove liners.

Socks should be in thin and medium weights that can be layered and will dry quickly. Buy socks that will wick moisture away from the foot (typically cotton/synthetic blends or Coolmax). Cotton socks are comfortable in very hot weather, but when they get wet, they stay wet and lose their insulating ability. If you like all-cotton socks, bring extras. Choose socks that match your activities. Thorlo makes socks for every imaginable activity, featuring extra cushioning in critical areas. For a little extra warmth and comfort, consider fleece socks (which double as slippers) and silk or modified polyester-knit sock liners.

Tights instead of hose keep you warm in cold weather.

You may want to invest in a lightweight, packable pair of galoshes to cover your shoes for rain, or, before you go, treat your shoes with water repellent to protect them.

Clothing Care on the Road

Plan on doing a little laundry every night or every other night instead of saving it all up. I wash underwear in the shower at night, hang them to dry, and they're ready by morning. This way, you'll need to take fewer clothes.

Check all garment labels for specific care requirements. Be sure to choose fabrics that are easily washed on the road. Always use a gentle soap (never harsh detergents) for washing. Clothes-washing items you might want to bring are listed on page 258.

Hand Washing Cotton, Silk, and Delicates

1. Fill the sink or tub with lukewarm water. Add travel soap or a cold-water detergent, such as Woolite.

2. Swish the garment (do not squeeze, twist, or rub it) for a couple of minutes.

3. Rinse thoroughly in cold water.

4. Lay the wet garment on a towel (a Packtowl is ideal for this), and roll it up to remove excess water.

5. Hang cotton, synthetics, and natural and synthetic blends to dry.

Hand Washing Wool and Other Sweaters

CAUTION: Wool takes time to dry except in very hot, dry weather.

1. Fill the sink with cool or cold water. Add a cold-water detergent such as Woolite.

2. Soak garment for three minutes.

3. Squeeze soapy water very gently through the sweater.

4. Rinse thoroughly in cool or cold water.

5. Roll the sweater in a Packtowl or ordinary towel to remove excess moisture. Do not wring or twist.

6. Dry the sweater flat. Block it to the original size if needed.

Removing Wrinkles

Hang out tomorrow's outfit to get the closet wrinkles out. Remember to take an extension cord and adapter plugs to use with your iron (and a converter if it is not dual voltage). Be sure the garments are cool and dry before wearing them. If they are still warm, the wrinkles will form again.

Ironing

Use an iron to add crispness to a garment (especially with cotton or linen) and to press creases in.

1. Turn down the bedcovers to create an ironing surface.

2. Test the iron heat on an underside, hidden edge of the fabric first. Synthetics take low heat; natural fibers take higher heat.

3. Press garments on the wrong side with a press cloth to prevent shine or scorch. (A large handkerchief or a used sheet of fabric-softener works as a press cloth and allows you to see what you are doing.)

4. If desired, use spray starch to keep cotton looking crisp.

5. Do not move or wear garment until it is completely cool.

Steam-and-Dry
This method makes wrinkles smooth out of dry clothes.

1. Hang one or a few sets of clothes in the bathroom.

2. Turn on the hot water in the shower or bathtub.

3. Wet your hand and glide it vertically down the garment, moistening the fabric.

4. When the shower is steaming or the tub is between one-third and half full, turn off the water. Remove silks and cottons (they should not be left to steam, because they are so absorbent) and close the door.

5. Leave the clothes hanging up for thirty minutes or up to two hours, depending on the fabrics. Wools, wool blends, and most synthetic blends steam out well, as do most linen and cotton blends.

6. Let clothes air dry before wearing them.

Travel Steamer
You can use a steamer to remove travel wrinkles and creases. Steamers are lighter than irons and can be used anywhere in the room where you can hang a garment—you need not create an ironing surface—but they cannot be used to press a garment. They work best on light and medium fabrics.

1. Hang garment from a door or window rod.

2. Fill the steamer as indicated, and wait about five minutes for steam to develop. (You can add a pinch of salt to hasten the process.)

3. Glide the steaming head along the garment, pulling and smoothing the fabric with the other hand as you go. Wrinkles should smooth out easily.

4. Make sure that you empty, rinse, and dry the steamer after each use, according to instructions.

Quick Method

Wrinkle-Free is a commercial fabric-relaxer spray that can be found in drugstores, travel stores, and luggage shops. It can remove wrinkles from almost all fabrics, except for 100-percent polyester. It is a spot treatment and works best on absorbent fabrics such as cotton, wool, and silk. To use, spray the garment, wait ten seconds, and smooth out the wrinkles by hand.

Shoes

The quest for comfortable travel shoes should equal your determination to travel light. Comfort has to be a top priority when you are purchasing shoes. Luckily, several manufacturers make wonderful-looking men's and women's shoes that combine good looks with comfort. Women: try to limit yourself to three pairs of shoes. I suggest bringing a dressy shoe (such as a low pump), walking shoes, and sandals or flip-flops. Men: one pair of all-purpose walking/dress shoes, along with a pair of sandals for hot weather, should suffice. In all cases, search for versatile, multipurpose styles. For example, Rockport makes walking shoes that are appropriate for all but the most formal occasions. Teva or Clarks sandals are also good walking shoes. Ecco Mobiles can be worn hiking and in the city, too. Other quality brands are Merrill, Timberland, SAS, and Easy Spirit.

A plethora of trendy yet comfortable sneakers have come on the market recently, in all colors and styles. Many are versatile enough to be worn anywhere, except a fancy restaurant. By the way, a pair of light rubber flip-flops are handy for beach and shower.

Recommendations

The Walk Shop in Berkeley, California, which specializes in comfortable shoes, has a number of recommendations:

- All shoes should have springy, resilient composition soles that cushion the step as you walk. Leather soles are usually too hard. Injection-molded soles form a permanent unit and are highly recommended.

- Look for thick soles with excellent traction and abrasion resistance such as those made by Vibram. They can be found on a variety of shoe styles for men and women.

- Because your foot changes size during the day, buy a shoe with an adjustable lace or strap.

- For tropical weather, look for open styles that allow your feet to breathe.

- Some shoes, such as those made by Mephisto, Clarks, and Ecco, have "air-conditioning," sophisticated airflow systems built into the sole to ventilate the foot.

- Some people need or wish to let their shoes dry completely between wearings. If you do, take an extra pair, or buy shoes, such as those made by Ecco or Rockport, that come with removable insoles that can be taken out and dried between wearings. Instead of alternating shoes, you can just change the insoles. Or buy Spenco removable insoles. For excessive perspiration, look for a lined shoe.

- Definitely take a pair of sandals for warm weather. Highly recommended are the three-strap, orthopedic-footbed sandal made by Clarks for women, or the Teva for men and women. These double as walking shoes. For men and women, Rieker makes a design that is part shoe and part sandal, with a T-strap.

- Make sure your shoes are big enough and fit properly. Try them on with the socks you intend to wear. Size numbers vary between manufacturers, so pay more attention to the fit than to the size number.

- Make sure that you wear your shoes at least six times before your trip. This gives you time to make necessary adjustments before you leave.

- Consider water repellency. Many types of walking shoes are now made with waterproof leather. If you need to treat your shoes, get an alcohol-based treatment (not a silicone-based one) for general travel. Silicone-based treatments seal the shoe completely and are recommended for hiking boots.

NOTE: All repellants will darken the leather slightly as they provide protection against rain.

Accessories

Accessories greatly expand the versatility of your travel wardrobe, enabling you to transform a simple day outfit into dramatic evening attire. The travel wardrobe is a simple, classic background—accessories will add variety, texture, and color. They take up little room and will be a cheerful addition to your wardrobe.

Scarves

☐ One large square or long rectangular shawl (at least 35 inches). This is the most versatile shape; it can be used to dress up a jacket, dress, or blouse. A shawl can be used as a head covering for religious sites, as an emergency blanket, and, in warm weather, will protect you from the sun or take the chill off in air-conditioned rooms. Consider the lightweight pashmina, or other comfy, compact shawls.

☐ One long rectangle. Use it as a sash or with a blouse.

☐ One square (at least 25 inches square). A large bandanna is a good all-purpose scarf.

Belts

Take one or two in leather or fabric in neutral colors, or take high-quality elasticized belts with one or two interchangeable buckles. A snazzy metallic belt is useful for eveningwear. Covered buckles will match jewelry of any color. Fabric belts are appropriate for casual garments and warm climates. Some belts have zippers in the back to hide money.

Jewelry

Keep it simple! Gold is universally appropriate, as are pearls for dressing up. Choose a few basic pieces: one pair of earrings that can be slept in, one pair of evening earrings, costume pearls, and a simple gold chain. But if you love jewelry, here is where you can splurge. Do not take anything of monetary or sentimental value; it is not worth risking the loss. If you do decide to bring valuables, carry them in your security wallet and deposit them in the hotel's safe deposit box. (Also see chapter 11 on security; not all hotels are trustworthy.)

Shoe Clips

Found in shoe departments, these clip-on decorations dress up pumps. You can also use clip-on earrings for this purpose.

Hose

Plain stockings are the norm for business, but you can use color and texture to spice up your outfits for casual or evening wear. If you wear anything other than regular sizes, plan on taking enough hose from home to cover your trip. Take clear nail polish to stop runs. Also, try prewashing your nylons—they won't run as quickly as new ones!

Purses

Women should take one *small*, packable purse with a long shoulder strap. Select a simple and slightly elegant style that is also appropriate for a dressy evening. This is for your comb, tissues, pen, glasses, and walking-around money. You can keep this packed and take it out for a night on the town.

Men can pack a waistpack if desired. Take it out when needed.

IMPORTANT: Neither purse nor waistpack should hold more than basic necessities, such as notebook, pen, glasses, tissues, lip balm, medications, and the like. A small amount of cash for the next few hours is all the money that you need. *All* your other valuables should *always* remain in your security wallet.

5

THE PACKING LIST

Making a packing list is the most important thing you can do to avoid under- or overpacking. The packing list serves as your tool to contemplate, visualize, select, and edit your choices concerning what clothing and gear you will take on your trip. There are so many choices and decisions to make that the more effort you put into making your packing list, the more effective your wardrobe will be on the road.

Try to start your list at least two or three weeks before your trip. The more complex your trip, the earlier you will need to start constructing your list. This gives you time to plan, shop, select, and refine your choices so that you will end up with a manageable load.

Making Your Packing List: Three Steps to Avoid "Just-in-Case" Syndrome

The following steps allow you to focus on the wardrobe and travel-gear requirements for your trip. (Also see appendix 4, Planning in a Nutshell.)

Step 1. Plan for Weather and Laundry Stops

Use your travel itinerary and weather information from the Internet, the Weather Channel, the newspaper, and the Itinerary Wardrobe Planner (see pp. 118–119) to predict the temperature range, rain forecast, and humidity levels for your destinations. This will help you decide how many layers to bring and what types and weights of fabrics you will need. Pinpoint lodging and laundry facilities to clue you in to what fabrics will be maintainable and how many items of clothing you will need, given your laundry schedule. On the day you arrive will there be a laundromat nearby? A washing machine? A dry cleaner? The less available laundry facilities will be, the more hand washing you'll have to do, which will impact your clothing choices.

Step 2. Analyze Your Activities

Use the Daily Activity Planner on page 120 to list clothing and gear needed for special events, sightseeing, outdoor and sports activities, and business meetings.

Figure out in advance how you will create outfits for any special situations. Try assembling various outfits, laying them out on the bed and adding accessories, shoes, and so on. Refine choices as needed, writing down any missing pieces to acquire later.

Step 3. Make Your Packing List

Fill out the Women's Packing List on page 121 or the Men's Packing List on page 122. Circle wardrobe items you'll need, then use the list as a shopping list for any pieces needed to complete your wardrobe. When you pack the item, check it off. If it doesn't all fit in your suitcase, adjust your wardrobe and redo your list.

Step 4. The Post-Trip Review

Immediately after your trip, review the list and, for future reference, cross out items you didn't need. You can also use it as an inventory for insurance purposes should your belongings get lost. Whenever possible, keep shopping receipts for this purpose. If you travel frequently, you might develop a "business trip" list, a "vacation" list, a "weekend" list, and so on. Keep the lists on your computer or in your suitcase.

Itinerary Wardrobe Planner

Day no.	Date	Day of the week	Destination and type of lodging
1			
2			
3			
4			
5			
6			
7			
8			
9			
10			
11			
12			
13			
14			
15			
16			
17			
18			
19			
20			
21			
22			
23			
24			
25			
26			
27			
28			
29			
30			
31			

Weather forecast				Laundry facilities
High	Low	Rain	Humidity	

Daily Activity Planner

Day no.	Date	Location		
	Morning activities	Afternoon activities	Evening activities	Other activities
Layer 1 Underlayer				
Layer 2 Clothing				
Layer 3 Outerlayer				
Layer 4 Extremities, shoes				
Accessories				
Gear				

Women's Packing List

Underlayer
- [ ] thermal underwear
- [ ] underwear
- [ ] bras
- [ ] garment shields
- [ ] hose
- [ ] leggings or tights
- [ ] nightgown or large T-shirt
- [ ] swimsuit
- [ ] active wear
- [ ] pareo or sarong

Clothing
- [ ] jacket #1
- [ ] jacket #2
- [ ] skirt #1
- [ ] skirt #2
- [ ] pants #1
- [ ] pants #2
- [ ] two-piece dress
- [ ] dress
- [ ] cardigan or sweater
- [ ] shirt #1 (long sleeved)
- [ ] shirt #2
- [ ] shirt #3
- [ ] shirt #4
- [ ] T-shirts
- [ ] shorts
- [ ] athletic, sport clothing
- [ ] other ____

Outerlayer
- [ ] raincoat or rainjacket
- [ ] rainpants
- [ ] parka
- [ ] windbreaker
- [ ] poncho
- [ ] umbrella

Extremities
- [ ] shoes, dress
- [ ] shoes, walking
- [ ] sandals
- [ ] slippers
- [ ] socks, dress
- [ ] socks, casual
- [ ] sun hat
- [ ] rain hat
- [ ] ear warmers
- [ ] gloves/liners
- [ ] sock liners

Accessories
- [ ] belts, day
- [ ] belts, evening
- [ ] bandanna
- [ ] scarves
- [ ] handbag
- [ ] necklace
- [ ] pin
- [ ] earrings
- [ ] bracelets
- [ ] watch

Men's Packing List

Underlayer
- [ ] thermal underwear
- [ ] underwear
- [ ] undershirts
- [ ] large T-shirt
- [ ] pajamas
- [ ] swim trunks
- [ ] active wear

Clothing
- [ ] jacket #1
- [ ] jacket #2
- [ ] slacks #1
- [ ] slacks #2
- [ ] slacks #3
- [ ] sweater
- [ ] fleece jacket
- [ ] shirt #1 (long sleeved)
- [ ] shirt #2
- [ ] shirt #3
- [ ] shirt #4
- [ ] shirt #5
- [ ] T-shirts
- [ ] shorts
- [ ] athletic, sport clothing

Outerlayer
- [ ] raincoat or rainjacket
- [ ] rainpants
- [ ] parka
- [ ] windbreaker
- [ ] poncho
- [ ] umbrella

Extremities
- [ ] shoes, dress
- [ ] shoes, walking
- [ ] sandals
- [ ] slippers
- [ ] socks, dress
- [ ] socks, casual
- [ ] sun hat
- [ ] rain hat
- [ ] ear warmers
- [ ] gloves/liners
- [ ] sock liners

Accessories
- [ ] belts, day
- [ ] belts, evening
- [ ] bandanna
- [ ] ties
- [ ] watch
- [ ] cufflinks

Tried-and-True Tips from My Audience!

- Wear your heaviest or bulkiest clothes and shoes on the plane.

- Take old underwear and socks and discard them as you go.

- Wear old walking shoes and discard them on the last day of your trip.

- Pack old clothes and give them away or discard them as you go to make room for souvenirs and new purchases.

- Don't pack too many T-shirts—buy them along the way.

- Sell your jeans!

- Leave appliances at home.

- Send off or give away paper materials as you go—paper is heavy.

- Take a vacation from make-up.

- Remove all excess packaging.

- As a last resort, and to concentrate on your resolve, pack your bag and walk a mile carrying it. If you can handle it, well and good; if it is too heavy, be ruthless.

6

HOW TO PACK YOUR SUITCASE

I n this chapter, I will show you how to pack each of the basic carry-on pieces using the Bundle Method. *Once you know how to make "the bundle," you can apply it to any 21- or 22-inch carry-on or 24-inch checkable suitcase.* This includes one-compartment suitcases, such as wheelaboards (with or without "suiter" feature), two- and three-compartment (three-zip) shoulder bags, and the convertible backpack. (A vertical travel pack, used for extensive hiking, may need to be modified to accommodate the body's center of gravity.)

For those of you who require business or larger wardrobes, or simply more room for gear, I have added instructions for packing a carry-on with folded shirts, packing a garment carrier, and packing larger, 26-inch and 29-inch (checkable) standard Pullmans. Included also are tips for packing your secondary tote or daypack and a duffel bag.

IMPORTANT: Do *not* pack valuables such as passport, cash, credit cards, traveler's checks, tickets, extra photos, documents, and prescriptions. These do *not* go in your purse, your waistpack, your carry-on, your briefcase, or any other piece of luggage, but *on your person*, under your clothes, in a security wallet—no ifs, ands, or buts about it. (See pp. 45–49.)

The Bundle Method

The Bundle Method is a packing system perfect for soft-sided luggage. It creates a cushioned, woven mass of clothing (the bundle) that does not shift and hardly wrinkles. It is more versatile than rolling or folding because it accommodates tailored clothing, such as skirts, slacks, and shirts or blouses, as well as the more casual T-shirts and pants. The bundle contains wardrobe items only. We will deal with travel gear later.

Two key features make the bundle an asset for any traveler. First, it is a single unit of clothing that takes up half to the entire space in a 21- or 22-inch-long carry-on or a 24-inch checkable bag. The bundle takes up the length and height of the bag, but not necessarily the entire space of the bag: one may either pack a bottom layer of items with the bundle on top, or one bundle can take up the entire space. In both instances, shifting is minimized: clothes move around less and are less likely to wrinkle. Second, the bundle has no sharp folds or creases, only soft, cushioned edges. The bundle is made up of layers of clothing wrapped around an inner cushion I call the core, which is a pouch containing lingerie, underwear, socks, and other accessories. Each item of clothing is cushioned; because there are no sharp creases, the clothes virtually do not wrinkle.

Before we pack anything, let's look at the bundle as it would appear after you have finished packing.

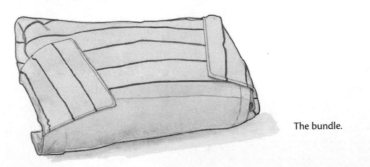

The bundle.

Packing It All In

Do not start packing until you have assembled every last item. Then read the directions for packing, right through, beginning with the next paragraph. There's more to packing than dumping stuff into a case and hoping you can shut the lid—but then you knew that, or you wouldn't be reading this book. I'll start with some general tips and then go on with detailed instructions for packing the different items of clothing.

Always start with the largest, heaviest, and longest items of clothing—typically a jacket or straight dress, but not slacks. First layer tailored clothing that is likely to wrinkle. Save knits and wrinkle-resistant items for the inner layers.

Align collars and waistbands flat along the edge of the bag, not pushed up against the sides.

The sequence of what goes in first varies for each person according to the size of the garments. Generally, large jackets and sweaters are laid down first, followed by smaller garments. This gives them more room to wrap around the core. Experiment with your clothes to find your appropriate packing sequence.

The Bundle Method does not require covering garments with plastic. However, if you have delicate fabrics that wrinkle easily, you can encase the garment in a plastic dry-cleaning bag. I usually use plastic only for hanging items in suiters or garment bags. For more on the use of plastic, see the discussions of the various packing methods that follow in this chapter, and pages 241–242.

Tissue paper can be rolled and stuffed into sleeves and under collars to decrease wrinkling.

Assemble the following packing aids:

- A core pouch, optional (see p. 134)

- Shoe covers—use fabric shoe bags or other shoe holders. Do not use plastic. Old socks can suffice.

- A plastic dry-cleaning bag (if you are hanging a suit in a wheelaboard suiter and a bag is not provided with the suitcase).

- A laundry bag—a polyester mesh laundry bag, a plastic bag, or a fold-up expandable tote. You can also use plastic compression bags. Another idea is the Sea to Summit Ultra-Sil Dry Sack, which comes in different sizes (see appendix 2, Resources).

The following are optional:

- Tissue paper
- Eagle Creek Pack-It Shirt Folder or similar model
- Tie case (long zippered case, or plastic cylindrical caddy, at Magellan's)
- One skirt hanger

Getting Started

Here are some general instructions. See below for packing specific types of suitcases.

Before you begin, clear a large space for packing, such as your bed or a large table. A clothing rack is a space saver for hanging wardrobe items instead of stacking them.

1. Put aside those clothes you will wear on the plane.

2. Make another pile of clothing and accessories you will want quick access to on arrival—for example, a big T-shirt, nightwear, workout clothes or swimsuit, shorts and a T-shirt, or a rain jacket. These are your "accessibles."

3. Gather your shoes. Stuff them with rolled-up socks, hose, and underwear. Place in shoe covers or plastic bags (do not seal).

   TIP: A woman's shoes can often be packed inside a man's pair to save space.

4. Gather belts, ties (with or without tie case), and scarves.

5. Gather underwear, socks, hose, and other wardrobe-related accessories and place them in your core pouch.

6. Have your travel kits on hand, packed in nylon pouches or plastic zip-locking bags. Also include hat, travel raincoat and umbrella, small purse, and appliances. We will get to these after we make the bundle.

7. Stack the rest of your wardrobe on the bed or hang it on a clothes rack. Button shirts and zip zippers. If you are using a hanging clothes caddy, hang the garments as they are listed, from left to right; if you are using your bed, stack them from the bottom of the list up, so that item number one is on top. Arrange as applicable.

Women
1. Long *straight* skirt or *straight* dress
2. Jacket
3. Straight skirts
4. Dress—A-line or full skirted
5. Skirt—A-line or full skirted
6. Slacks or split skirts
7. Shirts, long sleeved (with scarf, if any)
8. Shirts, short sleeved (with scarf, if any)
9. Sweater or other knits (if any)
10. Shorts

Men
1. Jacket
2. Slacks
3. Shirts, long sleeved
4. Shirts, short sleeved
5. Sweater or other knits
6. Shorts

Making the Bundle

Lay the suitcase on the bed. Open the deepest section completely so that the bag lies flat.

Pretend the base of your open suitcase is a clock face. Garments will be the "hands" of the clock—placed alternately in 12 o'clock, 3 o'clock, 6 o'clock, and 9 o'clock directions. We will be using the vertical orientation (from 12 to 6 o'clock) for jackets, shirts, straight dresses, and skirts. The horizontal orientation (from 9 to 3 o'clock) will be used for slacks, tri-folded items (full dresses and skirts, A-line skirts), and other narrow items like sashes.

NOTE: The "hinge end" is the wall of the bag that will touch the floor when the bag is put down. The "top end" is opposite from the hinge end, where the handle is.

Straight Dress or Straight Long Skirt (Illustration A)

For a straight dress, center the collar at the hinge end of the case so that the shoulders of the dress remain smooth. Place the shoulders in the corners. Make sure that the dress collar meets but does not bend against the wall of the bag. Smooth along bottom.

Now, drape the bottom of the dress over the opposite end of the bag (where the handle is). Drape the sleeves, if any, over the side walls of the bag. Smooth out the dress along the floor of the bag as best you can, lining the walls.

A. Straight dresses or straight long skirts, if any, go in first. Otherwise start with your jacket.

Jacket

This will be your first layer if you do not have a straight dress or long straight skirt. There are two ways to pack it.

Method 1 (Illustration B): Button the jacket and lay it in the suitcase face up. The collar should lie flat, flush with—but not bending up against—the hinge end of the case, to allow the width of the collar and shoulders to remain smooth (reverse direction when layering over a dress, as shown in Illustration B). Center the collar and hold it down using one hand. With the other hand, drape the bottom of the jacket over the handle (top) end of the bag. Drape the sleeves over the short sides of the bag. Use all of the space in the bag; get as close to the walls of the bag as possible.

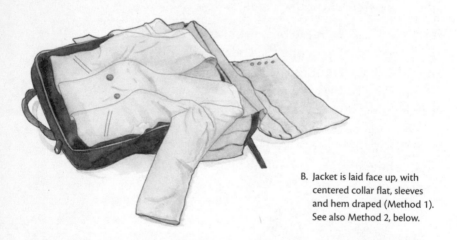

B. Jacket is laid face up, with centered collar flat, sleeves and hem draped (Method 1). See also Method 2, below.

Method 2: If the jacket is too wide or the sleeves do not drape easily, unbutton the jacket and lay it in the suitcase face down, with the collar flat, bringing in the lapels so that the width of the jacket fits the bag. Drape the bottom of the jacket over the handle (top) end of the bag. Bring the sleeves into the bag, laying them vertically down the jacket. Cushion the crease in the shoulder area if you wish. The fold will smooth out quickly when the jacket is worn.

Straight Skirts

Lay the skirt on top of the jacket, with the waistband at the opposite edge of the case from the jacket collar. Hold down the skirt with one hand and smooth it out with the other. Drape the bottom of the skirt over the opposite end of the bag. Add another skirt if desired, alternating waistbands.

A-line or Full-Skirted Dress

Keep in mind, full skirts and dresses are not recommended. If you must take one, you will have to fold it in thirds (tri-fold) before packing it. Lay the dress face down on a flat surface. Fold one side in, forming a straight vertical line. Fold the sleeve down vertically. Repeat for the other side. Now lay the dress in the bag horizontally, with the middle portion lying along the floor of the bag. Drape the shoulders over one side and the hem over the other.

A-line or Full Skirts (Illustration C)

These, too, you will have to tri-fold lengthwise and pack using the horizontal direction of the bag. Lay the skirt on the bed. Fold one side in a third, forming a straight vertical fold. Repeat on the opposite side. If you would like to cushion these folds, place some nylons, socks, or tissue paper in them to minimize the crease. Now, using the horizontal direction, lay the hem at one edge of the bag. Smooth the skirt, and drape the waistband over the opposite side. (Hems will wrinkle less if packed this way.)

C. Full skirts are folded lengthwise and packed horizontally. Place hem first, draping the waistband.

Slacks (Illustration D)

Match up the creases in both legs. Lay the slacks over the jacket (or skirts), bringing the waistband flush with the bag's narrow side. Smooth out the slacks and drape the bottoms over the opposite wall. If you have another pair, repeat the process, this time placing the waistband against the opposite edge.

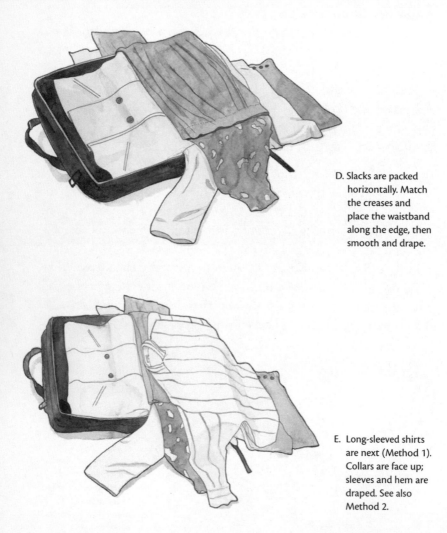

D. Slacks are packed horizontally. Match the creases and place the waistband along the edge, then smooth and drape.

E. Long-sleeved shirts are next (Method 1). Collars are face up; sleeves and hem are draped. See also Method 2.

Long-Sleeved Shirts (Illustration E)
Depending on the width of the shirt, use one of the two methods described below.

Method 1: Lay shirts or blouses face up in the bag as you did the jacket, making sure to alternate collars. Make sure the collars are flat and not pushing up against the side of the bag. Drape the sleeves and bottoms over the sides.

Method 2: If your shirt is wider than the suitcase, use the face-down method. Lay the shirt face down, with the collar centered. Vertically fold each side of the shirt so that the edges align with the side of the bag. Cross the sleeves over the back of the shirt. If needed, fold the sleeve ends across the side of the shirt. Drape the bottom. (If you prefer to pack folded shirts, see How to Pack Folded Shirts, p. 143.)

Scarves
If you have scarves, pack them as a layer next to the blouse you might be wearing them with. (Similarly, once you are familiar with the technique, try putting whole outfits together.) Or you can fold them into your core pouch.

Short-Sleeved Shirts (Illustration F)
Place them in the same way that you placed long-sleeved shirts. Lay them in the case, center the collar, and drape the bottom and sides over the walls of the case.

F. Short-sleeved shirts, T-shirts, and knits are next. Shorts are last. The core, containing underwear and other sundries, is placed in the center. The swimsuit can be put where it is appropriate for your needs—if you want easiest access, put it in with the accessibles. Otherwise it can be packed in the core pouch.

Now you are finished with all of the wrinkle-prone, tailored items. You have also reached the center of the bundle. Here is where you put knits such as sweaters.

Sweater

Place your sweater or other knits over the blouses. Drape the bottom and sides.

Shorts

Where you place shorts depends on their length. Match up the seams. For long shorts, use the vertical direction of the bag, adding them soon after the slacks. For short shorts, use the horizontal direction, adding them last.

Undershirts, Boxer Shorts, and Sleepwear

These can be folded neatly and placed in the center of the space. Or place your sleepwear on top of the finished bundle so that it will be accessible on arrival.

The Core Pouch

The core acts as the center cushion, supporting the layers of clothing you have just put in.

The Core (Illustration G)

The core is made up of a pouch (about 11 x 16 inches) containing your swimsuit and other small wardrobe items such as lingerie, undergarments, and socks. Sundry items such as jewelry can be

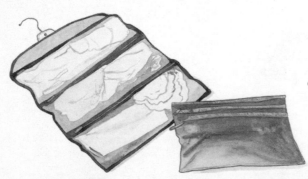

G. Samples of core pouches: these go in the middle of your clothing bundle. For the organizer on the left, tuck in hanger and fold pouch in half before packing.

packed here too. I recommend the Carry-rite 5-pocket Mini Orga nizer (#315) available at Easy Going and other luggage stores (see appendix 2, Resources). Do *not* use a plastic resealable bag for the core; it is slippery and will cause garments to shift.

Place the core in the center of the bag with about 2 inches of space all around it (Illustration F). Make sure that the edges are nice and full—the better the edges are built up, the less things will wrinkle. If you don't have a core pouch, simply place the items in the middle to fill an 11 x 16-inch space.

To Close the Bundle

The core will be wrapped by layers of the clothing that you draped over the sides of the bag. To begin, hold the hem corners of the last garment that was layered immediately below the core (Illustration H). Fold the hem up over the core, wrapping any leftover hem around and under the core. Then fold the sleeve across the core, wrapping any extra material around the curve of the core. Repeat for the other sleeve (Illustration I). Continue down through the layers, starting with hems, then sleeves, wrapping each around the core and smoothing out wrinkles (Illustration J). Pack as tightly as you can. Make sure you fold the bottom of the garment up first and then each sleeve; do not interweave garments with one another.

H. Close the bundle by folding in sleeves and hems. By smoothing as you go and packing tightly, you will end up with fewer wrinkles in your clothes.

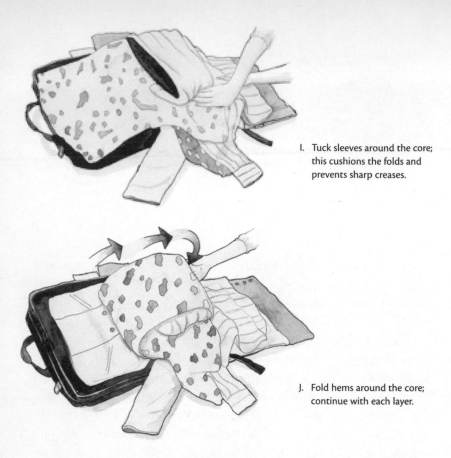

I. Tuck sleeves around the core; this cushions the folds and prevents sharp creases.

J. Fold hems around the core; continue with each layer.

After the last layer is folded over, secure the straps to keep your wardrobe in place. Do not cinch them too tightly.

Shoes

You have space for one pair of shoes in this section and one in the other section. Place shoe bags along the bottom of the case next to the bundle. If they are flat, place the heels in the corners of the bag with soles facing the hinge (Illustration K). Place high heels diagonally inward. The heel should not face the hinge or the clothing. If you have large shoes, try placing them with the toes at an angle or packing them below the bundle (see Packing a One-Compartment Suitcase, pp.141–143). You can also cut down on the number of pairs you take, or use accessory space or that second tote bag.

K. The finished bundle. Place shoes along bottom edge of bag; tuck belt around the zippered rim.

Belts

Line your belts along the inside zippered rim of the suitcase (Illustration K).

Ties

These can be handled in a number of ways. If you want nice, crisp ties, buy a tie case that fits the measurements of the bag and lay it on top of the bundle. You can also use a stiff piece of cardboard and wrap the ties around it, securing them with a rubber band. Also handy is a small round caddy that can be packed with your travel gear or in the corner of the case. Or, for that one tie you might use if you get into that four-star restaurant in Paris, simply wrap it around the finished bundle.

Accessible Items

Now take those items you kept out of the bundle for easy access. Lay these on top of the bundle or tucked into the corners outside of the bundle. Such items might include the next day's socks and underwear, a folded nightgown, a swimsuit, shorts and a T-shirt, or a sweater.

Alternate Packing Strategies

Sometimes impatience, lack of time, or lack of concern about wrinkling creates the desire for a slightly faster method of packing. Here are two shortcuts that I like. Experiment with them and see if you like one better.

Quick-Fix Bundle Method

This is perfect for on the way home. Lay all the items in the suit-case, with collars and waistbands stacked in the same direction. Drape all sides as you would if you were using the perfectionist's method. Place the core in the middle. Now take all the bottoms at once and fold them over the core, wrapping them around if need be. Do the same with the left sleeves. Voila! There is your bundle. The difference is that the outer edges are not as nicely built and the sides of the garments will wrinkle. But if you are in a hurry or on your way home, who cares?

Packing on Hangers—The Z-fold Method

This option is for packing suits, dresses, and other outfits in a carry-on suitcase (with or without suiter option), a garment bag, or even a duffel bag. The outfits are hung on wire hangers, encased in plas-tic dry-cleaning bags, and packed into the bag. The plastic reduces wrinkling by eliminating friction, making this the preferred pack-ing method when wrinkle-free clothing is a top priority. It is also convenient to arrive in the hotel and hang the clothes right up. The downside is that you cannot fit in as many items of clothing when you pack this way. The clothing cannot be packed too tightly without defeating the purpose.

Hang your outfit on one hanger: pants or skirt over bar, then shirt/blouse, then jacket. Pull the shirt sleeves through the jacket sleeves. Stuff with tissue paper if you like. Cross the jacket sleeves in front. Cover with a plastic dry-cleaning bag, and tuck in the hanger. Lay the shoulders of the jacket against the hinge end of the bag. Pick up both sides of the midsection of the jacket and bring the midsection up to the shoulders in a Z-fold. Tuck any hem underneath. Voila! The suit fits into your bag, and you're packed.

For bags with the suiter option, hook the hanger on the clip, lay out the jacket, and then do a Z-fold.

For a duffel bag, it's a bit different—put the outfits on hangers, roll each in thirds horizontally, and lay into the duffel.

Unpacking

When you arrive at your hotel, unfurl the bundle and let the garments drape over the sides of the bag. This will give them a chance to air out and relax. Hang them up if you will be staying a few days. You will find it is easy to insert the hangers while the clothes are still in the bag. Hang up the core pouch or put it in the drawer. To repack, you will not have to fold much, just lay the garments in quickly. Nor will you have to iron, so you will save even more time in the long run.

Getting Clothes In and Out

If you have packed only separates, it is easy to unfurl two or three garments, reach inside the bundle to grab the one you need, slip it out, and repack. If you have packed longer items such as a dress, you will have more to unwrap. This is another reason for packing separates only! Also, try to think ahead and keep the next day's underwear out as an accessible.

Packing Your Toiletries and Incidentals

Now the clothing is taken care of. What about toiletries, personal items, appliances, more shoes, small purse, raincoat, umbrella, and so on? Where you put these items will differ according to the suitcase you have. The following instructions are for packing specific types of suitcases. Find the one that applies to your luggage.

- Assemble all of your packed pouches, baggies, and so on

- Make sure to pack liquids and creams in tight, high-quality bottles. Fill three-quarters full, squeeze out air, and close. Wrap in plastic bags and store in organizer pouches away from clothing.

- Consider the placement of your gear according to the access you'll need during different phases of your trip. You'll probably be moving things around as you go. Some suggestions for placement follow. For more tips on accessories, see chapter 3.

Packing a Three-Compartment Carry-on with Two Wardrobes

The instructions that follow are for packing a 21- or 22-inch-long bag that has three full-length compartments, such as the Easy Going Special Edition Bag. This configuration is the most convenient for multipurpose and multiclimate trips because it allows you to organize your clothing according to purpose and season. The deepest section will hold your wardrobe bundle for business and cold weather, the second will hold a minimalist leisure and warm-weather wardrobe, and the third will contain all your other accessories.

NOTE: You need a core pouch for each separate bundle.

Section 1

Make a bundle with your dress or cold-weather clothes. Put the bundle in the deepest section of the bag.

Section 2

This compartment will hold casual or warm-weather items, if applicable. When you have a second wardrobe, make a separate bundle, arranging your casual jacket, skirts, slacks, long-sleeved shirts, T-shirts, and walking shorts, in that order. Assemble the related underwear, socks, and other wardrobe accessories in the core pouch.

Section 3

This compartment will hold all of your other accessories—everything that is not part of your wardrobe. Use this compartment for your packable raincoat and umbrella, toiletry kit, laundry kit, medical kit, collapsible bag, Packtowl, hairdryer, iron or steamer, water-purification items, flask, packable purse or waistpack (stuffed with odds and ends such as immersion heater, money exchange calculator, and so on), books and maps, and converter and adapters. Think of this space as four or five vertical columns, running from the bottom hinge to the top. This is an efficient use of the space.

Pack the columns in stacks from front to back, with flat items toward the middle and irregular shapes toward the outside. Pack all the heavy items at the bottom of the bag, with light objects on top. Because your toiletry or shaving kit is 14 or 15 inches high, it will stand in the suitcase vertically. Your packable raincoat and umbrella go here. Cushion objects such as hairdryers with the raincoat.

Packing a Three-Compartment Carry-on with One Wardrobe

If you have only one basic wardrobe, you will probably be able to fit all the garments into the middle section of the bag. This gives you lots of flexibility for using the other two side pockets. Put your accessories in one side compartment. In the other, you can put your dirty laundry, clothing (such as a sweater), items you want quick access to, extra shoes, or business papers.

Packing a One-Compartment Suitcase (21 to 24 Inches) with or without Suiter Option

Standard suitcases and wheelaboards have only one deep section. You can make a partition, making it a two-compartment bag. Popular suiter bags have a section in which you can hang a suit or jacket.

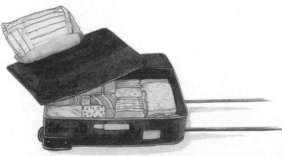

One-compartment bag, with accessories in bottom, then partition, then bundle. Accessibles are laid on top.

The best way to pack such bags is in three layers: a bottom layer made up of your accessories, irregularly shaped objects, and shoes; a middle layer made up of the bundle; and a top layer of the accessibles you want quick access to on arrival.

1. Open your suitcase. On the floor of the bag, place your personal items, appliances, laundry kit, first-aid kit, shoes, small purse (stuffed with kits or other items), water purifier kit, and so on. Heaviest items should go toward the edge that will touch the ground when the bag is put down.

   You can also roll up extra socks, T-shirts, leggings, and other soft garments to fill gaps and prevent items from rolling.

   You can use Pack-It cubes, pouches, baggies and the like here.

   TIP: To keep the accessories from moving about and to create a smooth surface for packing the bundle, buy a package of light- to medium-weight, nonwoven interfacing (the brand name is Pellon) at a fabric store. Each piece is 3 yards long by 22 inches wide. Cut a piece double the length of your suitcase and fold it in half. Lay it over the accessories, in effect creating a sectional divider. Tuck the edges down around the sides of the bag, enclosing the accessories and creating a shelf.

2. Make your bundle, as described on pages 129–138.

3. Lay your accessibles on top of the bundle. I might put in a big T-shirt, sleepwear, swimsuit, or sweater face up, fold both arms across horizontally, and fold the garment in half, bringing the bottom up to the shoulders. I lay a pair of walking shorts vertically.

4. For suiters, layer slacks or skirt over the hanger bar, then hang a shirt and layer the jacket over it, pulling the sleeves through. Cover it with a plastic dry-cleaning bag. To cushion folds, use the supplied cushioning bars or your own socks or rolled tissue

paper. Cross sleeves inward in front of the jacket and fasten the supplied straps across the jacket.

5. Outside pockets: depending on configuration, pack these with quick-access items and liquids (like medicine, makeup, toiletries), packable raincoat and umbrella, hat, water bottle, and items such as inflatable pillows, eyeshades, and earplugs to be used on the plane. Or pack with computer, business materials, and so on.

How to Pack Folded Shirts

Some people prefer to travel with folded shirts. You can pack shirts folded from the laundry, or you can fold your own.

Best for casual shirts is the Pack-It Folder by Eagle Creek, a packing aid that holds and compresses folded and stacked shirts.

For business travel, if you travel regularly with folded shirts, look for luggage that has a separate compartment for shirts. For example, Atlantic offers a suiter with a mesh compartment in the lid for shirts.

Here are two methods for packing folded shirts when using the Bundle Method of packing:

1. Follow item (1) of the preceding instructions.

2. Place folded shirts (or folder) in the bottom of the bag.

3. Make a small bundle of slacks, jacket, skirts, and the like.

4. Place bundle on top of the shirts.

5. For suiters, follow directions as above for hanging a jacket or suit.

Or you can use this method:

1. Put travel gear on the bottom of the bag.

2. Put your shirts in a Pack-It Folder on top of the gear.

3. Make a bundle on top of the folder.

Packing a Two-Compartment Carry-on

For the two-compartment suitcase, you do not need to make a divider. Typically the bag has a partition for organizing contents into separate compartments and is most suitable for a single-bundle wardrobe.

1. Pack section one, the bottom side, with accessories, irregular objects, and shoes as you would the one-compartment bag.

2. Pack section two, the top side, with the bundle and shoes.

3. Lay your accessibles on top of the bundle. Tuck socks and underwear into the corners of the bag.

Packing a Travel Pack (Convertible Backpack)

If you are using your travel pack as conventional luggage, you can pack it the same way you pack for a wheelaboard Pullman (see previous section).

However, if you will be using it as a pack for hiking or long-distance carrying, travel packs require a different technique because you have to take weight distribution into consideration. For general travel on gentle terrain, heavy items such as gear and shoes should be carried on top and closer to your back. Lighter items such as clothing should be packed toward the bottom and away from your back. However, if you are doing hiking and climbing, a lower center of gravity is needed. Pack heavy items in the middle, close to your back. Use clothing and the inside cinch straps to help keep the pack balanced and items in place. There are two ways to pack a convertible pack—the Bundle Method and the roll-and-stuff method.

Bundle Method

1. Make a bundle of your clothes, keeping aside what you want quick access to. Lay the bundle in the well of the bag toward

the bottom (the south end) near the waistband. Secure it with tie straps.

2. Nest one shoe inside the other and place the pair along the top edge of the bag (the north end; if you are carrying your bag vertically, this will be near your head).

3. Place accessories and kits at the north end of the bundle and around the top edges, using organizers such as color-coded stuff sacks or nylon pouches. Heavier items should be clustered toward the top edge, close to your back. Wrap items with a travel towel or some clothing to prevent shifting.

4. Place items you need to reach quickly, such as a rainjacket, on top of the accessories near the zippers (or hang on the outside of the pack). Also pack accessibles in outside pockets.

Roll-and-Stuff Method

1. Roll your clothes and place them in color-coded stuff sacks, one each for clean clothes, dirty clothes, city clothes, hiking clothes, and so on. Accessories can go into pouches, stuff sacks, or zip-locking bags.

2. Place lighter items, such as clothing sacks, at the south end of the bag. Place a jacket or sweater at the north end.

3. Place equipment and shoes at the north end on top of the jacket, away from the back. (If you are climbing and hiking, this is reversed—lighter items go higher and farther from your back, and heavier items go in the middle, closer to your back.)

4. Place items you need to retrieve quickly around the edge, in outside pockets and near the zippers. Always put things back in the same place, so you can find them in the dark and avoid forgetting things.

Packing a Garment Bag

First, here are some optional handy supplies to keep things in tip-top shape:

☐ Cardboard hanger extenders: available at good dry-cleaning stores. These give added support to suit shoulders on wire hangers.

☐ Plastic dry-cleaning bags: hang over suits, jackets, dresses. These reduce friction and let clothing drape naturally.

☐ Tissue paper: helps prevent the creases caused by folds. You can stuff layers of tissue paper under draped slacks and stuff collars and sleeves.

Here's the packing method:

1. If you have a cardboard extender, put it on the hanger.

2. Hang pants over the bar and a skirt on top of the slacks.

3. Hang a sweater or shirt on the hanger, then hang the jacket on top. Pull the shirtsleeves through. Smooth collars. Cross the sleeves in front of the jacket.

4. Cover with a dry-cleaning bag and hang in the garment bag.

5. Pack the hangers holding easily wrinkled items such as blouses and shirts toward the back of the bag to cushion the horizontal crease when the bag is folded in half.

Try to store the bag either hanging or lying flat.

Packing Larger (Checkable) Suitcases (24 Inches and Up)

Sometimes you have too many things to bring to limit yourself to a carry-on-sized bag, or you can't be bothered with carry-on. This means you can include (be more liberal with) items you'd have had to leave out of a carry-on.

The best way to pack a suitcase is in three layers: a bottom layer made up of your accessories, irregularly shaped objects, rolled items, and shoes; a middle layer made up of clothing; and a top layer of accessibles—anything you want quick access to on arrival.

1. Open your suitcase. On the floor of the bag, place your appliances, books, laundry kit, first-aid kit, shoes, gifts, small purse (stuffed with kits or other items), water-purifier kit, and so on. Heaviest items should go toward the edge that will touch the ground when the bag is put down. Fill spaces with rolled-up knits, T-shirts, leggings, hosiery, and other casual garments to fill gaps and prevent items from moving.

2. Layer 2: wardrobe items

   Method 1: Hang jackets, dresses, suits, and shirts together on hangers. Encase in plastic dry-cleaning bags. Use the Z-fold (see p. 138) or lay them flat in a 26-inch suitcase.

   Method 2: Use the interfolding method (if desired, cover each item with dry-cleaning bags):

   a. Using alternate directions (left and right), lay the upper half of long items such as slacks, dresses, and full skirts (folded vertically on each side) in the case horizontally. Drape bottom halves over the opposite side of the case. (If the case is very large, items can be laid flat.)

   b. Lay the upper half of sweaters, blouses, straight skirts, and jackets vertically in the case, draping the bottom of the garments over the edge. (This is the perfect place to stash breakable or fragile items!)

   c. Now flip the draped portions of the clothing into the case.

   d. Tuck socks, underwear, and other soft items around the edge where needed to fill spaces.

   e. Pack your coat on top, using the interfolding method.

3. Lay your accessibles on top of the bundle. I put in a big T-shirt, nightgown, or sweater, face up, fold both arms across horizontally, and fold the garment in half, bringing the bottom up to the shoulders. You might put a pair of shorts here, too.

Packing a Duffel Bag

By popular demand, here's how to pack a duffel bag. Duffels are best suited for casual clothing, although it is possible to roll up garments on a hanger encased in dry-cleaning bags and place them into a large duffel on top of heavy items. Always pack a duffel snugly. Fill the corners. You can get a lot into a small space.

Place heavy items (books, appliances, gear, shoes, and so on) along the bottom of the bag. Stuff shoes with socks and similar items and place in shoe bags. Roll T-shirts, knits, jeans, and the like, and make a layer of these. On top, place shirts, blouses, and sweaters folded once across the middle, sleeves folded inward. Or you can put these latter items on hangers in a plastic dry-cleaning bag and fold in thirds or a Z-fold (see p. 138). (These two layers can be interchanged, depending on which items you want to have accessible.) On top, place your raincoat or jacket. Drop the packed bag a couple of time to settle the contents.

Packing a Tote Bag or Daypack

Keep in mind the sequence of your needs when packing your second bag. This bag can bear more weight, as you will most likely put it under your seat and not overhead. To avoid losing items, try to return each to its proper place.

Outside Pockets

☐ boarding passes, customs documents, local currency, and any other items you need accessible for boarding and leaving the plane or train (with your passport, ID, and the like in your security wallet!); or use a boarding wallet.

- [ ] pen and notebook
- [ ] emergency items: knife, flashlight, umbrella, hat, tools, compass
- [ ] water bottle
- [ ] personal music player

Bottom

At the bottom, place valuables, clothing, and other necessities you will not need frequently.

- [ ] sweater or jacket
- [ ] umbrella
- [ ] keys
- [ ] camera and film
- [ ] half of your traveler's checks
- [ ] a change of clothing
- [ ] gifts
- [ ] breakables

Middle

- [ ] in-flight toiletry kit: moist towelettes, toilet-seat covers, tampons, mints, toothbrush and toothpaste, floss, comb, lip balm, moisturizer, headache reliever, Band-Aids, jet lag and motion sickness remedy, earplanes, and so on
- [ ] snack, water bottle

Top, Near the Zipper

- [ ] medicine, cup, water bottle, eyeglasses, sunglasses
- [ ] in-flight materials: laptop (fully charged), business papers, reading materials, maps, guidebook, and so on
- [ ] in-flight travel accessories
- [ ] thick socks or compression socks (such as TravelSox) for the plane

7

BUSINESS TRAVEL

Okay—you've read all the basics. Now let's put some wardrobes together for your next trip. Use these lists as guidelines to help you prepare for your trip. The sample packing lists are organized by layer because I believe that every traveler should get in the habit of thinking, "Do I have what I need for Layer 1? Layer 2?" and so on. (See chapter 4 for details on layering.) Provided are moderate, minimalist, and luxury packing lists. There are also simple packing lists for several types of business trips.

For businesspeople, carry-on luggage has many benefits. It gives you more control over your trip and schedule by eliminating the possibility of lost luggage and allowing you to avoid the carousel and get right to your hotel or meeting. Indeed, traveling light is an art form. Instead of lugging around three or four bags after you get off the plane, try to stay with one reasonable carry-on and a laptop or shoulder bag. This will make it much easier for you to board transit, visit offices, and stop off at restaurants or cafes. The lighter you travel, the easier it is for you to climb stairs and avoid wearing yourself out. A rolling carry-on bag is preferred for business travel, particularly when you have to head from a meeting directly to the airport or train station. You won't have to head back to your hotel to pick up your luggage. Can't figure out how to pare down business materials? Simply ship displays or samples ahead to your destination. They'll be waiting for you when you arrive. With airline baggage limits, it may be cheaper to UPS, FedEx Ground, or Priority Mail items ahead. Not sure you can trust the mail? Then consider a light backpack for those extra valuables. It will still be easier to move through turnstiles and revolving doors, and you won't have to wait around for a door person to ferry all your belongings.

Perfect appearance is often the highest priority for business travelers. For that reason, I recommend that you select your wardrobe fabrics carefully, choose the right luggage, and use plastic dry-cleaning bags as necessary to help combat wrinkles on the road. Of course, if your hotels offer twenty-four-hour clothing-care services and amenities such as irons, adapter plugs, hairdryers, and toiletries, you can pack less and still feel confident that you'll be able to maintain your appearance on the road.

In this section, I offer business wardrobes for different types of trips. Use the following guidelines to make leaving on a business trip routine.

Set Yourself Up for Success

Choose the right luggage. With the right bags on hand, you will be prepared for any type of trip. I recommend the following:

☐ A 22-inch wheelaboard suiter (with or without "portable office" features) or a three-compartment suitcase. Either of these will suffice for short trips with one or two jackets and coordinated separates (use a luggage cart if necessary). These are also great for vacation travel.

☐ A hanging garment bag (two- to four-suit capacity for longer trips and lots of clothes, or a simple, lightweight garment cover for that one tuxedo, suit, or evening dress).

☐ A smaller briefcase, shoulder bag, or small duffel for your glasses, toiletries, makeup, medicine, cell phone, laptop and computer accessories, iPod, MP3 player, headphones, work and reading materials, itinerary and travel documents, office supplies, water bottle, and spare shirt and underwear, in case your main bag is separated from you.

See chapter 2 for further descriptions of these bags.

Traveling with a Laptop Computer

Even though laptops are extremely portable, traveling with a laptop isn't as easy as it looks, especially for the international traveler. It pays to know all the issues before you decide to bring yours.

First, there's the weight issue. Invest in a lightweight laptop with a wireless card and a back-up battery pack, a charger, power adapters, ethernet cable (the cables you find in hotels often don't work), backup media such as a flash drive, CDs, DVDs, and various other equipment.

Second, be aware of your power needs—what it takes to plug in. In the United States most computers run on 110 volts, but if the foreign voltage is 220 volts, you will need a converter. You will also need the proper adapter plugs for the wall sockets. You can buy adapter plugs with or without grounding plugs.

Because it's easy to find wireless access in many regions, you may want to book hotels that have this preferred service. If you have a Skype account or Vonage's Soft Phone service, you can make and receive calls via your computer, saving money over hotel phone systems and most cell-phone plans. If you are traveling in an area that does not have wireless access, you can easily access your email at an internet café. It also helps to have a free Yahoo! or Hotmail account as a backup to your own email service. Visit www.teleadapt.com (see appendix 2, Resources) for more information on access abroad. Another source is www.warrior.com. Another good idea is to forward your home or office phone to your cell phone. This is easily done with Voice over Internet Protocol services such as Vonage.

Take lots of batteries or the extra battery pack if you have a flight longer than two hours. Future trend: some (usually long-haul) airlines are now equipping themselves with "laptop friendly" seats. You need an in-flight adapter, which will allow you to plug your computer into a 12-volt DC power supply built into certain airline seats. To find out more about this, contact Teleadapt and register with their Airpower Database. They will keep you posted on the adapter and also on all airlines and seats that offer airpower.

The Business Travel Wardrobe

Traveling for business requires careful focus. Your wardrobe must allow you to present the best possible image in all your activities yet still be travelworthy. If you will be moving around a great deal and meeting with different people, you can take the minimalist wardrobe, laundering as you go. If you will be seeing the same people constantly, you will require the moderate or luxury wardrobes. You may find a hanging suit bag necessary.

Here are a few guidelines to make business packing a breeze:

- Make a packing list. Take into account destination dress codes, climate, and activities (see pp. 88–100). Make a list of two or three completely accessorized outfits. They should all coordinate with each other. Use your list for each trip, then refine it for the next one.

- Keep your packing list(s) stored on your computer, and leave a hard copy in your suitcase for the next trip.

- Choose fabrics carefully. Invest in packable light- or medium-weight wool suits, merino wool or silk knits, cottons, cotton/polyester dress shirts and casual slacks, washed silk, and linen (see chapter 4 for more details).

- Stick to one or two coordinating neutrals. Make one a dark neutral that will be suitable for day or evening—black, navy, gray, or brown. The second should be a lighter, coordinating color such as white, gray, ivory, or khaki. Use accent colors, such as burgundy, red, and other brights, for shirts and blouses.

Shoes, belts, and handbags should be in your basic neutral colors.

- Try to pack items that can double for daywear and casual wear.

- Pack a dress shirt for each business day, up to five shirts. Choose high-quality cotton and polyester pinpoints and oxfords (available from Lands' End) if possible. Pack shirts hanging or folded, as you prefer (see chapter 6). All dress shirts are uncooperative to pack!

- Pack a pair of hose for each business day, plus a spare pair. Launder hose before wearing them to decrease likelihood of runs.

- Purchase thermal silk underwear in styles suitable for business attire if traveling in cold weather.

- Pack using plastic dry-cleaning bags, cardboard hanger supports, and tissue paper, available at dry-cleaning stores (see chapter 6).

- Always find out if your hotel offers twenty-four-hour laundry service, and amenities such as irons, adapter plugs, hairdryers, and toiletries. If they do, pack less!

- Pack slip-on garment shields to cut down on laundry.

- Always take a swimsuit or activewear for the hotel gym.

- Store valuables and money in a security wallet (see chapter 4).

Women's Business Travel Wardrobes

Business Suit Wardrobe for Women

This wardrobe is for the woman who wears suits during the day and has special dinners or other events in the evening. You'll see you can add to the minimalist basics to create a moderate or luxury version. All items should coordinate.

Minimalist

Layer 1: Underlayer

- [ ] 3 to 6 pairs of underpants (3 if you will wash, 6 if not)
- [ ] 2 bras
- [ ] 1 or 2 sets of garment shields
- [ ] silk-knit undershirt or camisole to wear under blouses if it's cold
- [ ] above-the-knee silk shorts to wear under skirts if it's cold
- [ ] 1 half-slip (optional)
- [ ] 1 extra-large T-shirt or cover-up for sleepwear and pool or pajamas or nightgown
- [ ] Swimsuit with cover-up (optional)

Layer 2: Clothing

- [ ] 1 suit
- [ ] 2 blouses (both day-into-evening)
- [ ] 1 two-piece dress that coordinates with the suit or 1 simple shirtwaist dress in a coordinating neutral tone

Layer 3: Outerlayer

- [ ] 1 raincoat and umbrella, if needed

Layer 4: Extremities

- [ ] 1 pair of walking pumps
- [ ] 1 pair of dress pumps for evening
- [ ] 3 pairs of hose for day (or 1 pair for each business day)
- [ ] 2 pairs of hose for evening (sheer)
- [ ] flip-flops for pool, if needed
- [ ] athletic shoes or sneakers, if needed
- [ ] athletic clothing and underwear, if needed

Accessories

- [ ] 2 scarves
- [ ] jewelry (earrings, brooch, necklaces)
- [ ] 1 evening handbag

Moderate
To the minimalist wardrobe add

- [ ] 1 suit
- [ ] 1 blouse

Luxury
To the moderate wardrobe add

- [ ] 1 two-piece dress or other dress, for evening wear
- [ ] 1 pair of evening shoes
- [ ] accessories for evening wear

Business-Coordinates Wardrobe for Women

Classic-looking coordinates are for women who do not need business suits but must look professional. All items should be day-into-evening styles. Pack the Business Suit Wardrobe (above), with the following substitutions to layers 2 and 4.

Minimalist
Layer 2: Clothing

- [ ] 1 simple jacket (unstructured type)
- [ ] 1 skirt, tailored style (or 1 pair of slacks)
- [ ] 1 two-piece dress or 1 chemise-type or shirtwaist dress
- [ ] 1 or 2 blouses (1 for day or evening)

Layer 4: Extremities

- ☐ 3 scarves (1 shawl, 1 long rectangular, 1 square) (optional)
- ☐ simple jewelry (gold, pearls, necklaces)
- ☐ 1 or 2 leather belts
- ☐ Day handbag (or use briefcase)
- ☐ Small shoulder bag for day or evening
- ☐ 3 pairs of hose for day (more if you don't want to wash)
- ☐ 2 pairs of hose for evening (sheer)
- ☐ 1 pair of walking pumps in a neutral color
- ☐ 1 pair of pumps for evening, if needed
- ☐ flip-flops for pool, if needed

Moderate
To the minimalist wardrobe add

- ☐ 1 skirt or 1 pair of slacks
- ☐ 1 cardigan sweater (V-neck, to wear alone and with other tops)

Luxury
For special events, add to the moderate wardrobe:

- ☐ 1 more jacket or 1 dress
- ☐ 1 pair of shoes for a special outfit
- ☐ accessories for a special outfit

Combined Business and Leisure Wardrobe for Women

Clothes for casual activities after your business trip are easily included in your carry-on bag. If you are on the move and need room in your suitcase, send your suits home by Federal Express or UPS after the meetings are over.

To the minimalist business wardrobes listed above, add the following for casual wear:

- [ ] 1 pair of casual slacks
- [ ] 1 pair of knee-length shorts (optional)
- [ ] 1 skirt (optional)
- [ ] 2 casual shirts, such as a matching blouse and tank top
- [ ] 1 pair of athletic or walking shoes
- [ ] 2 or 3 pairs of casual socks
- [ ] activewear for golf, tennis, and so on, as needed

Off-Site Business and Casual Wardrobe for Women

Sometimes at a week-long conference held at a resort, there will be business seminars or meetings during the day, one or two dressy events at night, and a company barbecue on the weekend. You will need clothes for a variety of situations, so spend some time planning your wardrobe. You will be seeing the same people every day, so you will probably want to take a few more clothes. "Casual" can mean a T-shirt and jeans; simply choose a neat and stylish version. Your best-looking casual clothing should be carefully chosen. The color scheme can vary—you might want brighter colors for a tropical resort and darker ones for a suburban off-site retreat. If you wear the suit or casual outfit on the plane, you should be able to pack this entire wardrobe in one carry-on suitcase and a shoulder bag. Or, if you prefer, use a garment bag. For this wardrobe, pack the Business Suit Wardrobe (pp. 154–156), with the following substitutions to layers 2, 3, and 4:

Layer 2: Clothing

- [ ] 1 jacket and skirt or a suit, dark neutral (for day meetings and evening)
- [ ] 1 skirt, khaki
- [ ] 1 pair of dark neutral silk slacks, for evening
- [ ] 1 plain light neutral blouse (day or evening)

- [ ] 1 accent-color blouse (day or evening)
- [ ] 1 two-piece dress in a print, suitable for day or evening
- [ ] 1 accent-color cardigan or sweater set
- [ ] 1 pair of khaki slacks (for the barbecue)
- [ ] 1 casual top (for the barbecue; can be half of the sweater set)
- [ ] 1 nice dress for evening (such as for a banquet)

Layer 3: Outerlayer
- [ ] 1 windbreaker, if needed

Layer 4: Extremities
- [ ] 2 pairs of casual socks
- [ ] 1 accent-color belt
- [ ] 1 pair of dark neutral pumps (business)
- [ ] 1 pair of accent-color loafers or oxford-type shoes (for the barbecue)
- [ ] 1 swimsuit
- [ ] 1 attractive cover-up
- [ ] flip-flops or light sandals for the pool, if needed

Accessories
- [ ] 3 scarves (1 shawl, 1 long rectangle, 1 square) (optional)
- [ ] simple jewelry (gold, pearls, necklaces)
- [ ] day handbag
- [ ] small shoulder bag for evening
- [ ] 3 pairs of hose for day (more if you don't want to wash)
- [ ] 2 pairs of hose for evening (sheer)

Men's Business Travel Wardrobes

Regular Business Wardrobe for Men

If you will be meeting with different people every day, you can keep your clothing to a minimum. If you are with the same people constantly, you will need a few more shirts and a second suit.

Minimalist
Layer 1: Underlayer

- ☐ 3 to 8 pairs of undershorts
- ☐ silk-knit thermal undershirt and bottoms to wear if cold
- ☐ 1 extra-large T-shirt for cover-up and sleepwear or 1 pair of pajamas
- ☐ swim trunks, if needed

Layer 2: Clothing

- ☐ 1 suit
- ☐ 1 pair of matching slacks (to double as casual wear)
- ☐ 3 to 5 dress shirts (3 if you send laundry out, or take 1 shirt for each business day)
- ☐ 1 or 2 casual shirts, such as polo type

Layer 3: Outerlayer

- ☐ 1 raincoat and umbrella, if needed

Layer 4: Extremities

- ☐ 3 to 5 pairs of dress socks (1 for each day of the trip)
- ☐ 2 ties, or 1 tie for each day of the trip
- ☐ 1 belt
- ☐ 1 pair of dress shoes

- [ ] 1 pair of athletic shoes, if needed
- [ ] athletic clothing (T-shirt, shorts, underwear, socks, nylon warm-up suit), if needed

Moderate

For trips of one week or more, to the minimalist wardrobe add

- [ ] 1 suit or a blazer

Luxury

If you are planning to take a garment bag, to the moderate wardrobe add

- [ ] 1 suit or tuxedo

Combined Business and Casual Wardrobe for Men

Try using patterned socks, motif ties, a patterned sweater, or sports shirts to bring variety into the wardrobe, which is based on a color scheme.

Layer 1: Underlayer

- [ ] 3 to 8 pairs of undershorts
- [ ] silk-knit thermal undershirt and bottoms to wear if cold
- [ ] 1 extra-large T-shirt for cover-up and sleepwear or 1 pair of pajamas
- [ ] swim trunks, if needed

Layer 2: Clothing

- [ ] 1 dark suit (optional in some settings)
- [ ] 1 navy blazer
- [ ] 1 dress shirt for each business day (at least one white) with ties
- [ ] 2 pairs of slacks: 1 gray, 1 khaki (the latter doubles as casual)

- [ ] 1 pullover or cardigan sweater (cordovan V-neck or crew-neck, print or pattern)
- [ ] 2 casual shirts (striped, patterned, or polo type)

Layer 3: Outerlayer
- [ ] 1 raincoat and umbrella, if needed

Layer 4: Extremities
- [ ] 5 pairs of dress socks (1 for each day of the trip if not washing)
- [ ] 1 belt, black
- [ ] 1 pair of dress shoes, black
- [ ] 1 pair of casual loafers or oxfords, cordovan
- [ ] swimsuit for pool, if needed
- [ ] athletic clothing (underwear, socks, and shoes), if needed
- [ ] cufflinks, tie clips, other accessories as needed

Security

Travelers on business trips can be targets for theft and terrorist crimes. If you are traveling internationally, it pays to avoid being identified as a business traveler. Carry inconspicuous softsided luggage. Briefcases and computers should be kept with you at all times and packed inconspicuously. Pack your backup disks separately from the computer for extra security. Keep an especially close eye on your belongings as you go through security! For more about this subject, see chapter 11.

Checklist for Business Travel

- [ ] security wallet and contents (see pp. 45–51)
- [ ] cell phone, charger

- [ ] laptop bag, briefcase, sample case, luggage cart
- [ ] computer components, chargers (see pp. 77–78)
- [ ] PDA, smartphone, personal organizer
- [ ] pager
- [ ] business cards
- [ ] calculator
- [ ] notepad, pen, business stationery, envelopes
- [ ] expense ledger
- [ ] business papers, files
- [ ] itinerary
- [ ] frequent flyer, rental car, discount, gym membership vouchers and cards
- [ ] confirmations and vouchers
- [ ] convention preregistration and name tags
- [ ] other office supplies (see pp. 76–77)
- [ ] travel steamer or iron (dual voltage with adapters for foreign travel)
- [ ] mints
- [ ] other _____

8

ACTIVE TRAVEL AND ADVENTURE WARDROBES

In this chapter you will find simple packing lists for leisure and adventure vacations. If you are planning to devote your trip to climbing Kilimanjaro or biking the Maine coast, you will, of course, want to mix and match your lists. Leave heavier items at your base location that you can pick up at the end of your outdoor journey, assuming that you are making a circular trip. Blended trips that have both big-city and outback travel require careful planning. It may make sense to pick up a few items at your destination, such as beach mats or a broad-brimmed hat that protects you from the sun. That's one less item to carry on the plane.

Let's start with the Basic Moderate Carry-on Wardrobe. For the "moderate" packer, which includes most of us, eight to ten basic garments will create more than twenty different looks. It is basically one week's worth of clothing. If you figure that you will do laundry once a week with a hand wash in between, this wardrobe is good for any length trip, from one week to one year! You determine what the style will be—very casual, semicasual, or dressy. Vary bottom pieces according to your preference. All pieces should coordinate.

For more on building a travel wardrobe, see chapter 4.

The Basic Moderate Carry-on Wardrobe for Women

The basic nine or ten garments are as follows:

- [ ] 1 jacket (blazer or casual)
- [ ] 1 skirt that coordinates with the jacket
- [ ] 1 pair of slacks that matches or coordinates with the jacket
- [ ] 1 extra bottom piece—skirt or pants (casual)
- [ ] 1 long-sleeved shirt
- [ ] 2 additional shirts or blouses
- [ ] 1 outfit suitable for both casual and dressy occasions: a two-piece dress (a blouse and skirt made of the same fabric, which can be a print) with a matching belt or sash, or a skirt or slacks and blouse, or a simple dress
- [ ] 1 cardigan sweater

Believe it or not, this moderate wardrobe can be worn in at least fifteen different ways.

A Sample Packing List: Women's Moderate Wardrobe

Your packing list for a moderate wardrobe, organized by layer, would look like this.

Layer 1: Underlayer

- [ ] 1 or 2 T-shirts (in cold weather, substitute a long-sleeved turtleneck)
- [ ] 1 extra-large T-shirt for sleepwear or to use as a cover-up in warm weather or 1 set of thermal silk or polyester-knit long underwear (for cold weather)
- [ ] 2 to 8 sets of underwear (4 or 5 is average)
- [ ] 1 or 2 sets of garment shields
- [ ] 1 half-slip, if needed

- ☐ 2 bras
- ☐ 1 swimsuit

Layer 2: Clothing

- ☐ 1 coordinating jacket, skirt, and pair of slacks
- ☐ 1 pair casual slacks or skirt
- ☐ 1 two-piece dress or 1 simple dress or 1 blouse and a pair of slacks or 1 skirt and a blouse
- ☐ 1 or 2 blouses, shirts, or blouse-type sweaters; at least 1 long-sleeved shirt
- ☐ 1 cardigan sweater
- ☐ 1 pair walking shorts (optional)
- ☐ athletic clothing and underwear, if needed

Layer 3: Outerlayer

- ☐ 1 raincoat or windbreaker

Layer 4: Extremities

- ☐ 4 or 5 pairs of hose
- ☐ 4 or 5 pairs of thin to medium-weight socks (fast-dry or moisture-wicking)
- ☐ 2 pairs of sock liners
- ☐ 1 pair of dress shoes (low pumps or dressy flats)
- ☐ 1 pair of sandals or flip-flops
- ☐ 1 pair of walking or athletic shoes
- ☐ sun hat, rain hat
- ☐ gloves, if needed

Accessories

- [ ] 1 or 2 belts
- [ ] 2 or 3 scarves (1 large square shawl, 1 large square, 1 long rectangular)
- [ ] simple jewelry (a few basic pieces but nothing valuable)
- [ ] 1 umbrella

The Minimalist Wardrobe for Women

The minimalist wardrobe is ideal for short or warm-weather trips. It can be adapted for business or casual wear. If you like, add a pair of walking shorts.

Here are the basic six or seven garments, which can be mixed and matched however you like:

- [ ] 1 jacket or cardigan
- [ ] 1 matching skirt that coordinates with the jacket
- [ ] 1 pair of slacks that matches or coordinates with the jacket
- [ ] 1 long-sleeved shirt
- [ ] 1 more bottom piece
- [ ] 1 outfit suitable for both casual and dressy occasions: a two-piece dress (a blouse and skirt made of the same fabric, which can be a print) with a matching belt or sash, or a simple dress or a skirt or a pair of slacks and a blouse

To make a packing list for the minimalist wardrobe, use the one provided on pages 165–166 for the moderate wardrobe, substituting these basic garments for Layer 2.

The Luxury Wardrobe for Women

The luxury wardrobe will give you the most variety (and the heaviest bag!). It is an expansion of the moderate wardrobe with the addition of one to three items for evening wear, repeated business affairs, or special events. If the fabrics and colors of the extra garments coordinate with all the others and are suitable for day or evening wear (silk, wool crepe, rayon blends), your wardrobe will expand exponentially.

Choose one of the following additional clothing items or groups:

☐ 1 additional jacket

☐ 1 suit with a blouse (that coordinates with your other clothing)

☐ 1 two-piece dress with a jacket

☐ 1 blouse, 1 pair of slacks, and a cardigan

☐ 1 special-event outfit

You are taking only *one* additional outfit, not all five—you still plan to carry on your bag! For the suit, select a solid color or a tweed that coordinates with the original three-piece outfit. Make the extra blouse a different style from what's in the moderate wardrobe.

To make up a packing list, use the one provided for the moderate wardrobe.

The Basic Moderate Carry-on Wardrobe for Men

For the moderate packer, this is an eight- or nine-piece basic travel wardrobe. Use it for trips of any length between one week and one year, in varying climates, and for diverse activities. Men's clothing is, on average, larger and bulkier than women's, so this wardrobe may be the most that you can pack in a carry-on. Limit the number of garments by selecting versatile styles in compact, packable fabrics.

The basic eight or nine garments are as follows:

☐ 1 suit or a jacket with coordinating slacks

- [ ] 1 or 2 additional pairs of slacks that coordinate with the jacket
- [ ] 2 short-sleeved shirts
- [ ] 2 long-sleeved shirts
- [ ] 1 dark, thin-knit, medium-weight sweater

A Sample Packing List: Men's Moderate Wardrobe

Here is a sample packing list for a moderate wardrobe, organized by layer.

Layer 1: Underlayer

- [ ] 2 T-shirts (1 extra-large for cover-up/sleepwear, or add pajamas)
- [ ] silk or polyester thermal underwear (for cold weather; this can double as sleepwear)
- [ ] 2 to 8 sets undershorts, depending on how frequently you plan to wash them
- [ ] 2 to 4 undershirts, if desired
- [ ] 1 pair of swim trunks

Layer 2: Clothing

- [ ] 1 jacket and 1 pair of slacks or 1 suit
- [ ] 2 pairs of slacks for day or evening
- [ ] 4 shirts, at least 2 long sleeved
- [ ] 1 pullover sweater (V-neck is the most versatile)
- [ ] 1 pair of shorts (optional)
- [ ] athletic clothing and underwear, if needed

Layer 3: Outerlayer

- [ ] 1 raincoat or rainjacket

Layer 4: Extremities

- [ ] 2 to 7 pairs of dress socks
- [ ] 2 to 7 pairs of athletic socks (thin, medium-weight, drip-dry)
- [ ] 1 pair of walking or athletic shoes
- [ ] 1 pair of dress shoes
- [ ] 1 pair of sandals or flip-flops
- [ ] sun hat, rain hat
- [ ] gloves, if needed

Accessories

- [ ] 1 belt
- [ ] 1 or 2 ties
- [ ] cufflinks and handkerchiefs, if needed
- [ ] umbrella

The Minimalist Wardrobe for Men

The minimalist travel wardrobe is perfect for short or single-purpose (for example, strictly business or strictly casual) trips. You will be washing clothing fairly often. Vary the sleeve lengths according to climate and style.

The basic six garments are as follows:

- [ ] 1 suit or 1 sport jacket with 1 pair coordinating slacks in a neutral color, or 1 medium-weight V-neck or crew neck sweater with coordinating slacks (you may not need a jacket for a casual trip—a sweater and your rainwear may be sufficient)
- [ ] 1 additional pair of pants that coordinates with the suit or jacket
- [ ] 2 long-sleeved shirts
- [ ] 1 short-sleeved shirt (polo-type knit shirts are versatile)

To make a packing list, follow the preceding list for the moderate wardrobe, substituting your six garments as Layer 2. Add a pair of shorts if you want.

The Luxury Wardrobe for Men

You will need a second bag or a suit bag for the luxury wardrobe. Add to the moderate wardrobe *one* of the following outfits:

- [ ] 1 suit
- [ ] 1 jacket and a pair of slacks
- [ ] 1 sweater and a pair of slacks
- [ ] 1 special-event outfit

A Trip to Europe

A two- or three-week trip to Europe involves visits to big cities, side trips to country villages, perhaps a beach resort, and religious sites. On a trip of this length, it's likely to rain at some point. In the city, you want to be stylishly casual during the day with an occasional dressy look for evenings. Long sightseeing days require clothing that can transition easily from day into evening. Yet you will also need comfortable, casual clothing for day hikes, dress-down days, and the beach. Layer versatile, simple separates that are very comfortable. Solid colors are best. Black and white with an added bright color is a versatile color combination. Important accessories include a day bag large enough to contain a change of shoes, shirt or blouse, scarf, and jewelry for quick changes, plus a raincoat and umbrella. Also, don't forget to wear your security wallet at all times.

NOTE: If your style is more casual, take all casual items and one dress-up outfit, or see the Adventure Wardrobe (see pp. 178–181). To travel extra light, take only three bottom pieces. For summer heat, take Supplex nylon, cotton, cotton blends, and linen; for winter cold, take midweight wool and wool blends. Make sure your shoes are comfortable!

European Travel Wardrobe for Women

Citywear

- [ ] 1 jacket (loose blazer type)
- [ ] 1 cardigan sweater
- [ ] 1 pair of casual slacks
- [ ] 1 pair of nice slacks
- [ ] 1 simple skirt
- [ ] 2 T-shirts (my favorite is jewel neck, for versatility)
- [ ] 2 blouses (1 slightly dressy one to go with nice slacks)
- [ ] 1 slightly dressy two-piece dress, simple dress, jumper, or skirt and blouse
- [ ] 1 pair of dress shoes
- [ ] 1 pair of walking shoes
- [ ] 1 extra-large T-shirt for cover-up, sleepwear; or pajamas
- [ ] 2 to 3 pairs of socks (4 to 5 for winter)
- [ ] 2 to 3 pairs of hose or tights
- [ ] 4 to 5 pairs of underwear
- [ ] 2 bras, garment shields
- [ ] 1 scarf (a sash can double as a head cover or belt)
- [ ] jewelry (1 pair earrings you can sleep in, 1 nice pair for evening, plus simple pieces)
- [ ] 1 small purse for evening
- [ ] 1 packable raincoat/umbrella if rain is expected

Beachwear

- [ ] 1 swimsuit
- [ ] 1 pair of shorts (khaki walking shorts or knit pull-ons)

- [ ] 1 T-shirt or tank top (try to match with the skirts for additional versatility)
- [ ] 1 pair of flip-flops or sandals
- [ ] 1 sun hat

Also bring these travel-gear essentials: security wallet, Pack-towl, fold-up tote bag for beach and wardrobe changes, and picnic kit.

European Travel Wardrobe for Men

Citywear

- [ ] 1 jacket (blazer, casual, or rainjacket)
- [ ] 1 sweater (medium-weight, thin knit)
- [ ] 1 pair of comfortable, casual pants
- [ ] 1 pair of all-purpose dressier slacks (such as khakis)
- [ ] 1 pair of walking shorts or 1 more pair of casual slacks (lightweight)
- [ ] 2 polo-type knit shirts
- [ ] 2 long-sleeved shirts (at least 1 white)
- [ ] tie(s)
- [ ] 1 pair of walking shoes
- [ ] 1 pair of dress shoes (optional if walking shoes are all purpose)
- [ ] 1 extra-large T-shirt for cover up, sleepwear; or pajamas
- [ ] 4 to 5 pairs of socks
- [ ] 4 to 5 pairs of underwear
- [ ] belt
- [ ] 1 packable raincoat/umbrella if rain is expected

Beachwear

☐ 1 pair of swim trunks

☐ 1 T-shirt

☐ sun hat

☐ flip-flops or sandals

Also bring these travel-gear essentials: security wallet, Pack-towl, expandable tote, and picnic kit.

Beach/Resort/Cruise Wardrobe

Hawaii, the Caribbean, Mexico, here we come—sunshine by day, partying by night. Prepared with a simple mix-and-match wardrobe, you don't have to overpack.

On a cruise, there are plenty of opportunities to shop on the ship and in port, so it is almost impossible to be without a necessity. A basic wardrobe of lightweight shorts and tops for the day, a few nice casual outfits, and a couple of compact evening outfits or a tuxedo form the framework for your "traveling light" packing plan. Keep in mind that you can rent tuxes and gowns on board, which can allow you to take one carry-on. If you do pack them, you'll probably need a garment bag.

Important cruise gear includes a daypack or tote stocked with a change of clothes and personal items, because your luggage may take a while to get to your cabin; swimsuits and a nice cover-up for the pool areas (a pareo is great here); security wallet and phrasebook for shore excursions; antacid and elastic waistbands to compensate for the midnight buffets; and hat, water bottle, sun-protective sunscreen, shirt, and insect repellent for warm weather or tropical cruises. An umbrella and windbreaker and workout wear for the gym will also come in handy, as will a nightlight for the cabin. For Alaska and adventure cruising, any weather is pos-sible. See Cold-Weather Travel (pp. 181–182) for packing tips.

For tropical weather, see pages 182–184. Make sure to bring your binoculars!

If a resort is your destination, you'll want to find out about specific dress codes. You also need to think about packing sports equipment. If it is at all possible, try renting equipment once you arrive so you don't have to lug it. Call ahead to find out what people wear on the tennis courts and in the restaurant, and pack accordingly.

For beach trips, include a Packtowl instead of a cotton terrycloth towel, and bring a waterproof security wallet (see p. 48).

Women

- [ ] 1 sweater
- [ ] 1 cotton skirt or culottes
- [ ] 1 pair of lightweight pants
- [ ] 2 pairs of shorts
- [ ] 1 jumper or sleeveless shift
- [ ] 3 T-shirts (vary the styles—jewel neck, tanks, three-quarter-sleeve)
- [ ] 1 lightweight long-sleeved shirt for sun protection
- [ ] 1 or 2 compact evening outfits
- [ ] 2 swimsuits
- [ ] pareo or attractive cover-up
- [ ] 1 shawl or sash scarf
- [ ] 1 windbreaker and windpants
- [ ] compact workout wear
- [ ] underwear
- [ ] bras
- [ ] cotton socks, hosiery

- ☐ 1 pair of walking or athletic shoes
- ☐ 1 pair of walking sandals
- ☐ 1 pair of evening shoes or strappy sandals to wear with evening outfits
- ☐ sport clothing and equipment

Men

- ☐ sweater
- ☐ 2 pairs of lightweight slacks
- ☐ 1 to 2 pair shorts
- ☐ 2 button-down short- or long-sleeved shirts
- ☐ 2 knit shirts—polo type
- ☐ 1 pair of swim trunks
- ☐ pajamas or extra-large T-shirt for sleep
- ☐ windbreaker
- ☐ blazer/shirt/several ties (optional)
- ☐ 1 pair athletic/walking shoes
- ☐ 1 pair sandals
- ☐ 1 pair dress shoes and socks
- ☐ sport clothing and equipment
- ☐ underwear
- ☐ for cruises, add 1 tuxedo

Weekend-Getaway Wardrobe (Women and Men)

For this casual three- or four-day trip, you don't need much!

- ☐ 1 casual jacket

- [ ] 1 sweater or vest (knit or fleece)
- [ ] 1 skirt for women
- [ ] 1 pair of pants
- [ ] 1 pair of shorts
- [ ] 1 blouse or button-down shirt
- [ ] 2 T-shirts (one extra-large for nightshirt or swim cover-up)
- [ ] swimsuit
- [ ] sneakers or other comfortable shoes
- [ ] comfortable flats or pumps
- [ ] 3 or 4 pairs of light- and medium-weight socks
- [ ] 2 to 4 pairs of underwear

For cold-weather adjustments, see page 181–182.

Adventure Travel

Bags packed for physically active vacations or trips to less developed countries are far more likely to contain stuff taken "just in case" than are those packed for business travel, when the agenda is set in advance and amenities are readily available. Packing for an adventure trip or active vacation requires you to weigh self-sufficiency against the need to travel light. The need for self-sufficiency increases if you travel in areas where such things as medications and clean water are not available. Also, you must be prepared for various microclimates (such as those of jungle basins or mountaintops) during a single trip. Then, if your itinerary includes visits to cities, you will need "civilized" clothing as well, taking into account local dress codes.

What follows is the Basic Adventure Wardrobe with weather adjustments for cold, trekking and high altitudes, and wet or humid and dry or desert climates. Fast-drying, high-performance clothing is mandatory because active vacations bring one face to face with the elements and produce lots of laundry, too. A basic travel gear checklist is also included.

Women's Basic Adventure Wardrobe

This wardrobe is suitable for any warm-weather, on-your-own trip, such as a trip to Asia. If cool weather is expected, select heavier fabrics and follow the suggestions in Adjusting for Weather, Climate, and Type of Trip (starting on p. 181).

Minimalist
Layer 1: Underlayer

☐ 2 or 3 T-shirts

☐ 4 pairs of underpants

☐ 2 to 3 bras

☐ 1 pareo, sarong, or large T-shirt (for sleeping, lounging, and cover-up)

☐ 1 swimsuit (one-piece)

Layer 2: Clothing

☐ 1 lightweight cardigan

☐ 2 long-sleeved shirts

☐ 1 pair of cool, comfortable, loose-fitting slacks (look for those sold as "hiking pants")

☐ 2 travel skirts, midlength, lightweight cotton or cotton/synthetic blend with pockets

☐ 1 pair of knee-length walking shorts with pockets

Layer 3: Outerlayer

☐ 1 lightweight raincoat, nylon poncho, or windbreaker, with hood

Layer 4: Extremities

- [ ] 1 pair of walking shoes—these can be running shoes, light-weight walking shoes, or sturdy walking sandals. If you want a closed shoe for hiking in jungles or rivers, you will need a second pair of walking shoes that can get wet.

- [ ] 1 pair of sturdy sandals—these can be "super sandals," such as Tevas, if you plan to be in rivers, reefs, beaches, or other wet places; otherwise, Clarks orthopedic sandals are great.

- [ ] 1 pair of canvas shoes (espadrilles) or light sandals for dress (optional)

- [ ] 4 pairs of light- or medium-weight socks, fast-drying

- [ ] 4 pairs of lightweight socks (such as sock liners) in polyester (such as Capilene) or a silk knit

- [ ] 2 bandannas (1 large for sun protection)

- [ ] Hat—for sun, take a wide-brimmed style, preferably one that will protect your neck and ears. A baseball cap is also fine; be sure to also use sunscreen.

Moderate

To the minimalist wardrobe, add

- [ ] 1 outfit for the city: short-sleeved camp shirt and skirt or a cool shirtdress

- [ ] 1 T-shirt

- [ ] sashes, belts

- [ ] jewelry, simple beads, and earrings

- [ ] 1 pair of espadrilles or sandals for the city

Luxury

To the moderate wardrobe, add

- [ ] 1 outfit for the city

This will probably push you over the edge for one carry-on; avoid it if possible.

Men's Basic Adventure Wardrobe

This wardrobe is suitable for any warm-weather trip. See guidelines for cool-weather changes, starting on p. 181.

Minimalist
Layer 1: Underlayer

☐ 2 T-shirts (polo style)

☐ 2 to 4 pairs of underpants (Coolmax is the best)

☐ 1 pair of swim trunks (shorts can double as trunks)

☐ 1 large T-shirt (for sleeping, lounging, and beachwear)

Layer 2: Clothing

☐ 1 lightweight sweater

☐ 2 long-sleeved shirts with pockets

☐ 2 pairs of cool, comfortable, loose-fitting trousers with pockets (those sold as "hiking pants" are good)

☐ 1 pair of walking shorts, knee length, with pockets

Layer 3: Outerlayer

☐ 1 lightweight nylon poncho or windbreaker, with hood

Layer 4: Extremities

☐ 1 to 2 pair of walking shoes—these can be running shoes or lightweight walking shoes; if you want a closed shoe for hiking in jungles or rivers, you will need a second pair of walking shoes that can get wet.

☐ 1 pair of sturdy sandals—these should be "super sandals," such as Tevas, if you plan to be in rivers, reefs, beaches, or other wet places; otherwise, any open, comfortable shoe is fine.

☐ 4 pairs of fast-drying, moisture-wicking, lightweight socks

- [ ] 2 pairs of sock liners (Capilene)
- [ ] 2 bandannas, 1 large
- [ ] hat—for sun, take a wide-brimmed style, preferably one that will protect your neck and ears. A baseball cap is also fine; be sure to also use sunscreen.

Moderate
To the minimalist wardrobe, add

- [ ] 1 jacket

Luxury
To the moderate wardrobe, add

- [ ] 1 outfit for the city (slacks and shirt)

This will probably push you over the edge for one carry-on; avoid it if at all possible.

Adjusting for Weather, Climate, and Type of Trip

You may need to adjust the fabrics, number of layers, and shoes depending on the conditions of your trip. Consider the following suggestions in selecting your adventure wardrobe.

Cold-Weather Travel

- Take warm wool or fleece socks and sock liners.
- Add two pairs of underpants, as they will dry more slowly.
- Add thermal long underwear, cotton tights, or leggings.
- Substitute a pair of heavier-weight slacks for the shorts.
- Take a turtleneck instead of a T-shirt.
- Substitute a wool or microfleece button-down, long-sleeved, shirt or pullover for the light long-sleeved shirt.
- Substitute a fleece jacket for the cardigan.

- Pack warm shoes instead of open shoes.

- Add a warm hat and gloves.

- Make use of compression bags to pack bulky items.

Trekking or Mountain Travel

If your trip includes a trek to high altitudes, add the following to the adventure wardrobe. Try to rent most equipment and heavy clothing at your destination.

☐ long underwear (medium weight)

☐ anorak

☐ down parka or vest (rent it at your destination if possible)

☐ fleece jacket

☐ waterproof raingear

☐ lycra ski tights

☐ lightweight, weather-sealed hiking boots (do not rent these; wear them onto the plane to save suitcase space) or, for the tropics, ankle-height, fabric hiking boots

☐ 2 pairs each of thick, quick-drying socks and sock liners

☐ wool or fleece hat

☐ mittens or gloves (optional)

☐ sneakers

Tropical Travel

Humidity, intense sun, periodic rain, and cold at high altitudes are marks of the tropics. You need high-performance outdoor gear that dries quickly. Sunscreen, lip balm, mosquito repellent and/or netting, and anti-itch remedies are essential.

For tropical travel, take the Adventure Wardrobe and follow the following guidelines.

Clothing

Choose lightweight garments that will protect you from the sun and insects. Clothes should be loose fitting in a weave that helps ventilate the body. T-shirts should be of 100 percent cotton or a cotton/polyester blend. Fast-drying rayon and other technical T's are available, too. Mesh polo-type T-shirts are good because they protect the neck from the sun and are more versatile than plain T-shirts are. Long-sleeved shirts can be of cotton/polyester blends. A combination of 55 to 65 percent cotton and 35 to 45 percent polyester makes a good fabric. Patagonia makes one called Fishing Gear; Ex Officio makes the Baja Shirt and the Wayfarer. Patagonia also makes an A/C line of clothing especially for humid weather. Tarponwear and RailRiders also have an excellent line. (See appendix 2, Resources for more information.)

Ideally, skirts, slacks, and sport jackets can be of easy-care fabrics made of Supplex nylon, polyester/cotton, cotton/nylon, or tropical-weight wool/polyester blends. Spandex gives clothing an added measure of comfort. Women may want to bring a cool shirt-dress for city wear. Underwear should be of quick-drying synthetics or synthetic blends such as Coolmax. Shorts are not acceptable in all areas—check before packing them. You may want to consider a conservative, knee-length style with lots of pockets in a quick-drying cotton/nylon blend. Take a sun hat and chiffon scarves or bandannas to keep the sun off your head. If you have time to shop, hats, scarves, and sarongs will often be available at your destination. Plan on washing one item while the second dries, and buy everything in fast-drying fabrics. Excellent manufacturers are Ex Officio, Sierra Designs, TravelSmith, Royal Robbins, Tarponwear, RailRiders, and Early Winters.

NOTE: In Asia and in Muslim countries, women's wardrobes should be modest.

Shoes

In humid climates, shoes will get very sweaty and heavy. Mildew is a constant threat. It may be slightly harder to consolidate and wear the same shoes all the time. Try to limit yourself to three pairs of shoes.

If you are going to be in wet places such as rivers, jungles, beaches, and caves, take a pair of "super sandals," such as Tevas, which provide excellent support and remain comfortable when wet.

Take a walking shoe with a removable insole, choosing a lightweight, open-weave model. For the tropics, avoid leather because it is too heavy and does not dry.

The second pair should be a sturdy, comfortable sandal or walking shoe. For this you could use your Tevas or a supportive sandal such as those made by Clarks. You will wear these every day for traveling and walking. Women may want a lightweight pair of espadrilles or sandals for dress.

Desert Travel

Desert trips are characterized by dry, sunny weather with lots of wind, dust, and possible rain. The nights are cool. Desert gear should include a dustproof bag for your camera, eyedrops, such as Visine, for dust, Solarcaine or aloe vera if you burn, a wide-brimmed cap or hat, one or two large bandannas for dust, spare sunglasses, and, if you wear contacts, extra eyewash, lens cleaner, and glasses or goggles to protect against dust.

If on safari, choose comfortable clothing for long days spent riding in vans. There probably won't be much city travel. Depending on your destination and the time of year, you may need extra layers for warmth or rain. Take the Basic Adventure Wardrobe, with the following changes:

☐ 2 to 4 T-shirts

☐ 2 long-sleeved shirts (1 light for sunny days, 1 warmer for cool evenings)

☐ 2 pairs of pants, 1 in cotton or cotton/polyester twill; 1 in lighter weight, such as cotton/nylon, cotton/polyester sheeting, or Supplex nylon

- [ ] 1 windbreaker/rainjacket
- [ ] 1 warm fleece jacket or sweater for cold nights (optional)

Summer Hiking/Cycling/Hosteling Travel

Bring a super-light wardrobe for a summer of hosteling and hiking or cycling. For cycling, take cotton or Coolmax underwear and three pairs of socks, and substitute sturdy walking or cycling shoes for the hiking boots. If you want to dress up in the city, add one simple nice outfit. Take the Basic Adventure Wardrobe with the following changes:

- [ ] 1 long-sleeved shirt instead of 2
- [ ] 1 all-purpose wool or fleece sweater instead of a light cardigan
- [ ] 1 pair of slacks and 2 pairs of shorts (no skirts)
- [ ] 1 waterproof rainjacket and pants or poncho
- [ ] 2 pairs of hiking socks and 2 pairs of sock liners
- [ ] sturdy, comfortable hiking boots instead of walking shoes
- [ ] light sneakers for wearing around camp

Gear for Adventure Travel

For details on all items, see chapter 3.

- [ ] security wallet for carrying valuables
- [ ] daypack with lock: for carrying cameras and lenses, water bottle, rain gear, and so on. Small pockets are useful for film, sun cream, and sunglasses. Look for padded shoulder straps and waistband. In rainy weather, line the pack with a heavy-gauge garbage bag.
- [ ] convertible pack. The zipper should lock. In rainy weather, line the pack with a heavy-gauge garbage bag.

- [ ] expandable nylon tote bag: for storing city clothes at the hotel or in a locker while in the field
- [ ] luggage locks and tags
- [ ] personal prescriptions, medications, antibiotics (if necessary)
- [ ] first-aid kit with small booklet, IAMAT doctors list (see appendix 2, Resources)
- [ ] malaria pills, if needed, antidiarrheal and headache remedies
- [ ] iodine tablets or water-purification equipment (see pp. 58–59)
- [ ] water bottle: a wide-mouth bottle if bringing drink mixes
- [ ] pocket knife, compass, pocket mirror, tool kit, matches, tweezers
- [ ] tool kit
- [ ] sunglasses and retainer strap (get glasses that offer good UV protection)
- [ ] insect repellent; mosquito netting (headnet or other), if desired; mosquito itch aid
- [ ] sunscreen or sunblock cream with a Sun Protection Factor (SPF) of 15 or higher
- [ ] lip sunblock with an SPF of 15 or higher (such as Chapstick 15, A-Fil, or Labiosan)
- [ ] headlamp, Beam-and-Read light, or flashlight: for reading or writing in your journal at night
- [ ] 2 sets of extra batteries and bulbs (if you read at night)
- [ ] toilet paper, without the cardboard tube
- [ ] packtowl or a small, thin towel
- [ ] sewing kit
- [ ] bandanna
- [ ] travel umbrella

- [ ] travel alarm or watch with alarm
- [ ] journal, stationery, and pen
- [ ] toiletries kit: toothbrush and toothpaste, biodegradable shampoo and soap, deodorant, skin moisturizer, nail brush, nail clippers, small packages of tissues and towelettes, razor, shaving cream, baby powder, laundry soap, and adequate supplies of sanitary items
- [ ] spare eyeglasses and spare prescription sunglasses or clip-ons as a back-up; eyeglass straps. Contact lenses can be worn successfully, but be sure to bring a sufficient supply of solutions, including in-the-eye lubricants. An eyeglass-repair kit is also handy.
- [ ] camera equipment—water resistant is best.
- [ ] safety outlet plugs

9

TRAVELING WITH KIDS

No doubt about it, when traveling with kids, checking your luggage is way easier than carrying everything on the plane. Still, you will need to be mobile at your destination, so you need to pack as though you are going carry-on! The strategy is threefold: choose luggage and equipment that enhances your mobility, make every person as self-sufficient as possible, and abandon the notion that you take everything with you. A few well-chosen garments, snacks, toys, books, and tapes will be all your family needs to keep going. Although kids under two do not need a ticket, your best bet is to buy babies and small children their own seat. Not only is it more comfortable for the parents, but you can take advantage of the children's carry-on allotment! If this is not an option, check with your airlines about their carry-on regulations.

To be really good to yourself, take advantage of the services that deliver cribs, equipment, food, diapers, and supplies to your hotel door around the world! (See appendix 2, Resources.)

Luggage

Choose a luggage and equipment configuration that will enable you to balance bags and kids as you negotiate airports, planes, and crowds. The convertible backpack/daypack system works best for parents and kids age six and older (between three feet, six inches and five feet, two inches tall). Kids can easily carry their own luggage on their backs or pull a kid's wheelaboard. Small children between the ages of three and five can pack a small daypack with their belongings. Make sure it complements your luggage, as you may end up carrying it!

Kids have lots of options for luggage, just like adults. In the travel-pack department, Tough Traveler makes an ergonomically safe line of backpacks for ages five through adult. The Super Padre packs have all the trappings of other intermediate-level travel packs, but sized down—including control straps, mini internal frame, sternum strap, and thick, padded waist belt. There are four sizes, including a 22-inch pack that is carry-on size.

Skyway makes a nice line of traditional luggage for kids. There is a wheeled suitcase and a duffel as well.

Tutto makes the colorful Gizmo line of kids' luggage and daypacks. My kids each have one, and these packs are great! The 20-inch, four-wheeled suitcase pulls or pushes along easily with a U-shaped pullbar and can also be used as a seat or loaded with other extras. All the luggage pieces feature reflective tape on the outside. The external frame is incredibly sturdy, and the bag collapses to $2^1/_2$ inches for easy under-the-bed storage. Two-wheeled wheelaboards for kids are also appearing in the marketplace, but none with the adult quality of Tutto's wheeled bags.

When traveling with babies and small children, parents will find that the convertible pack enables them to travel hands-free to hold the children and a car seat, or to push a stroller. A baby front- or side-carrier can be worn at the same time. Or one parent might carry the child in a backpack-type child carrier while carrying a suitcase that has a shoulder strap or towing a wheeled bag. An additional umbrella stroller may be added if you have several small children. If necessary, a sturdy luggage cart, such as the Remin Concorde III, will carry numerous bags easily.

Take an expandable nylon suitcase that folds up into a small pouch. You will find a hundred purposes for this bag. The best one is that, if your carry-on allotment is limited in number, you can pack your baby's belongings in your own carry-on and then whisk out the expandable suitcase and transfer baby's gear while settling in for your flight.

All children, including infants, require a passport for foreign travel. Keep passports, money, traveler's checks, and tickets in a security wallet worn underneath your clothing. Two parents can divide multiple passports between them. A parent traveling alone with several children should wear two wallets to store valuables. Include prescription photocopies for medicine (for yourself and for your child), copies of your children's medical information, and the phone number of your pediatrician and health insurance plan on your address list. (The checklist on pp. 48–49 details the items that should be safeguarded in your security wallet.)

Instead of carrying a big purse, keep a small change purse or a nylon zip bag or wallet in the diaper bag for access to cash. A waist-pack will also work (but do not use it for valuables).

Self-Sufficiency

Make each family member as self-sufficient as possible. This increases a child's sense of participation and lessens the burden on parents. Let each kid (ages three and up) carry his or her own daypack with a light jacket or sweatshirt, bottle or cup of juice, snack, a personal tape player, and a few favorite books, toys, and tapes. One parent can keep a cabin bag with a backup stock of food. A waistpack is also useful, especially if the child is already carrying a backpack. Make sure to pack a lightweight daypack in the suitcase, though, for day hikes and excursions.

Security

Losing your child in a crowd is the scariest thought for parents. There are a couple of tools you can use to help keep them around you. The first is the simple wrist/waist reins. Keep it in the child's pack and designate it as a "special" thing just for the airport. Another alternative is the Angel Alert Child Distance Monitor. The child wears a small transmitter and the adult wears the receiver. An alarm sounds if the child wanders a little too far from adult. The Child's transmitter includes a panic button (www.family onboard.com).

Food

Hungry children are no fun on the road. Make sure each child is equipped with a water bottle and snacks. Apples, grapes, and other fruit that does not drip or stain, dried fruit, crackers, cereal or bagels, granola bars, trail mix, and cheese-and-cracker packs are good choices. Get kids into the habit of drinking plain water when they are thirsty, and you eliminate the constant need to buy or deal with juices that can stain clothes.

For bottle-fed babies, you should have enough for regular feedings and for two more meals in case you get delayed. Toddlers and small children should have finger foods in sandwich bags. Consider bringing a bag lunch on the flight if your child is a picky eater. Food may not always be available at baby's feeding times, and toddlers may not like what is served. (You can request "baby" and "toddler" meals from the airline in advance.) Juice and water are usually available on the flight.

Takeoff and landing are good times to give children a bottle or let them nurse or suck on candy. This will help alleviate possible ear pain caused by changes in air pressure. Or use Children's Ear-Planes (see Special Accessories for Kids, p. 202).

Entertainment

Choose items carefully for their portability and value. Simple items that rely on children's creativity, manipulation, and imagination will outlast items that stimulate superficially. I find that books and story cassette-tape sets are the best form of entertainment (after

Mom and Dad, that is). You can buy and trade books along the way and have them sent to you during a long trip. Make sure to bring a book with the words to songs, activities, and fingerplay. Below I list several practical and entertaining items for each age group.

For Babies (Pack These in Your Flight Bag)

- ☐ 2 or 3 board books (vinyl are especially light)
- ☐ rattles, especially those with moving parts, or dangling things such as plastic keys or measuring spoons
- ☐ a soft cloth ball
- ☐ teethers (such as a toothbrush)
- ☐ nesting objects
- ☐ mirror (use your pocket mirror)

For Toddlers (Pack These in Your Flight Bag)

- ☐ a favorite comfort toy or doll
- ☐ a "bag of tricks"—a purse or sandwich bag with odd things they are not normally allowed to play with, or a plastic seven-day pill dispenser filled with raisins and cereal (the child will be busy for hours opening and closing the caps)
- ☐ picture books and cassette tapes
- ☐ a book of songs so a parent can sing to them
- ☐ finger puppets
- ☐ art materials: crayons and paper; a small paintbrush and "paint with water" coloring books
- ☐ Duplos

For Small Children Over Three Years Old (Pack These in Their Own Pack)

- [ ] storybooks with cassettes to be used with a Walkman or headphones

- [ ] small box of art materials: paper and paper bags, string, pipe cleaners, blunt scissors to practice cutting, scotch tape

- [ ] an erasable travel slate (look for the lighter cardboard type)

- [ ] activity book and crayons

- [ ] portable dolls and play figures

- [ ] Legos

- [ ] small cars or a small pouch of microcars

- [ ] a small, divided plastic pill box useful for collecting small things, which kids love to do

For Older Children (Pack These in Their Own Pack)

- [ ] Walkman with tapes and headphones, or a microcassette recorder for recording stories, chronicling the trip, and so on

- [ ] book; a tiny atlas

- [ ] art materials: paper, blunt scissors, gluestick, sketch pad, colored pencils, sharpener

- [ ] journal and pens

- [ ] small travel games (magnetic checkers, electronic games, etc.)

- [ ] cards (get a small book of card games so you can play all kinds)

- [ ] camera and film

- [ ] crafts (for example, string and beads for making necklaces, needlepoint, crocheting)

Packing Kits

I like to pack kits for kids: a diaper kit, a medical kit, and a food kit. Invest in durable, zippered, nylon pouches. An insulated, foldable, six-pack bag with a shoulder strap is also handy for carrying food items.

The Diaper/Flight Bag

Let's assume you are allowed one bag for baby and/or toddler. A sturdy, high-capacity bag accommodates diapers, wipes, several changes of clothes, books and toys, four bottles or cups in insulated pockets, and up to eight jars of baby food. Include a zippered foldable pouch for baby's toiletries (I use this to make the small diaper kit), a removable zippered pouch for wet and soiled items, a compact changing pad, and a front pocket for the parents' stuff.

Any large daypack or tote will also serve this purpose, especially if you also have an insulated six-pack, lunch, or bottle bag for bottles and food.

Basic Diaper-Bag Checklist

☐ diaper changing supplies

☐ comfort toy

☐ books and toys

☐ medicine

☐ clothing

☐ food

To go into more detail, the diaper/flight bag should contain the following items.

An In-Flight Diaper Kit

This is incredibly handy. It can be pulled out of the diaper bag effortlessly and passed back and forth between parents. After changing baby, restock the bag immediately for your next use. Use any easily identifiable zippered nylon pouch measuring about 7 x 12 inches, and fill it with the following:

- [ ] 1 diaper*
- [ ] 1 pack of wipes (a travel-sized package or a zip-locking bag filled with wet wipes)
- [ ] 1 rubberized lap pad
- [ ] 1 compact vinyl changing pad
- [ ] 1 small tube of diaper-rash cream
- [ ] 2 plastic bags for soiled diapers.

Further items for the diaper/flight bag are as follows:

- [ ] 3 or 4 diapers/pullups
- [ ] resealable plastic bags in quart and gallon sizes, or a roll of sandwich bags
- [ ] pack of baby wipes
- [ ] 2 wet travel washcloths in separate resealable plastic bags— 1 for washing hands and faces, 1 as a mop-up cloth for tables, chairs, and so on
- [ ] nursing pads

Add the following, if needed:

- [ ] 2 all-purpose burp or nursing-cover-up cloths—use thin gauze-type cloth diapers, Packtowl, or thin flannel receiving blanket (these dry fast)
- [ ] extra nursing shirt, if worn
- [ ] waterproof drop cloth—disposable Lammies or a 1-yard square of vinyl to be used for protecting beds, too

---

* The remainder of your diaper supply (enough for the first leg of your trip) should be distributed in your suitcases, tucked into corners, or lining edges. You can also use your expandable nylon tote for diapers and stow it away as they are used up.

☐ toiletry kit: small bottles of liquid baby soap (which doubles as soap and shampoo), powder if used, baby sunscreen, toothbrush, and baby nail clippers

☐ stain pretreatment and soil remover—along with cold water, this is good for preventing stains from setting on washables

☐ all-purpose blanket—one compact blanket for baby to play or sleep on, or for use as a nursing cover-up. Can also be a tablecloth for picnics or used to create a play area for all kids (I use a thinly quilted cotton/polyester style).

Clothing for the Diaper/Flight Bag

☐ 2 outfits, including one for arrival—pack comfortable, nonbinding separates, and include booties if baby is barefoot

☐ 1 lightweight sweatshirt or nylon jacket with hood

☐ sun hat

Food

This can be consolidated in the diaper bag or carried separately in an insulated cooler bag.

☐ finger food: dry cereal, crackers, bagels for baby and older children; cheese-and-cracker packs, fruit leather, raisins for older children

☐ baby food: dehydrated, 3-ounce jars, or ready-to-serve microwave meals for babies older than five months

☐ plenty of moist towelettes

☐ a small plastic bowl with lid

☐ spoons: 2 sturdy plastic spoons (put long feeding spoons in a toothbrush container)

☐ bib—laminated or pack of disposables (Lammies)

☐ bottles: one for juice or water and one for formula, or take disposable liners; nipples, rings, and caps. (The First Years makes a nipple adapter so that you can fit any nipple onto disposable-liner bottles.)

☐ formula: ready-to-feed and dry, in a zip-locking bag. (One method is to fill a 1-cup plastic container with powder and scoop. Keep the container and a bottle filled with water in the food bag to mix when needed. Replenish after use. Maya makes a pre-measured, three-feedings cup. Use a pack that you preheat and wrap around the bottle to keep fluids warm.)

☐ a spill-proof travel cup (if appropriate)

Medical Kit

Add the following items to your own first-aid kit (see pp. 61–62) or put them in a place where baby cannot get to them.

☐ phone number of your pediatrician and IAMAT phone number (see appendix 2, Resources)

☐ prescription medications and vitamins for baby (try to get those that do not need refrigeration)

☐ Syrup of Ipecac for accidental poisonings (administer only with medical advice)

☐ medicine dispenser

☐ digital thermometer

☐ baby acetaminophen

☐ anti-diarrheal medication (ask your doctor)

☐ children's decongestant

☐ insect repellent (low dose [17.5%] DEET for kids) and an anti-sting or anti-itch treatment, such as calamine lotion, Benadryl, or 1% hydrocortisone cream

☐ EarPlanes, child size

☐ safety outlet plugs

Clothing Basics

Use the rules for grown-ups when packing for kids.

- Pack as minimally as possible, taking into account your laundry schedule. Try the "wash-one/wear-one" strategy, plus minimal backup. If you wish to do laundry only once a week, you will need to add clothing.

- Choose a color scheme for mix and match. All pieces should coordinate. This makes it easier for kids to dress themselves.

- Pay extra attention to layering. Babies and kids are especially at risk in cold weather. Each item of clothing should function as part of a layering system, complete with a moisture-wicking inner layer, insulating layer(s), and an outer layer. Do not forget to protect the extremities with hats, gloves, mittens, balaclavas, and so on.

- Pack separates—they are more versatile and layer easily. They also make diaper changing easier. Add a couple of sleepers for infants.

- Choose easy-care, fast-drying fabrics in various light and medium weights. Denim should be limited to soft, lightweight overalls that dry quickly.

- Choose dark colors and prints whenever possible—these conceal stains (this is useful for the parents of small kids, too).

Packing Tips

Older kids and teenagers can use the Bundle Method. Put a packing list in their luggage for repacking so that they will not forget anything.

For smaller kids, roll outfits together so they can easily unpack and dress themselves. (If everything is color coordinated, any choice they make will be presentable.) You can put rubber bands around the bundles or put them in plastic bags, if you like.

Keep the nice outfit (including shoes, socks, and hair accessories) in a plastic bag or stuff sack.

Set aside one play outfit (such as sturdy overalls) for getting really dirty—the rest should then remain relatively clean.

Appoint one person to carry all the swimsuits in a stuff sack, another the pajamas, and so on. This will speed up unpacking.

Clothing for unticketed babies and toddlers may have to go in a parent's suitcase. Lay the clothes neatly on top of the bundle or in one section of your suitcase.

Laundry

Each person can carry his or her own soiled clothing in a stuff sack. Pack-it Compression Bags are large plastic zip-locking bags. You put in the wet or soiled clothing, zip it up, then roll, pressing hard, so that the air comes out the other end. This will result in a "shrink-wrapped" bag of dirty laundry, which will be compact enough to fit in your luggage. I also use mesh laundry bags and regular plastic bags.

To prevent stains, ban popsicles, powdered drink mixes, and gelatin desserts, which contain dye; mustard; and dark red fruits and fruit juices from your menu. Carry a pretreatment spot-and-stain-remover stick along with a flask of water to prevent stains from setting until you can launder them. (For clothing care tips, see pp. 108–111.)

Layering Strategies for Children

Because of their small size and activity habits, children are more at risk for cold than adults are. Patagonia, a clothing company that makes functional layering pieces for babies, children, and adults offers this advice.

Babies and Toddlers

Babies have less insulating fat than older children have. They are also fairly sedentary, being carried in a pack or stroller. Dress babies and toddlers (up to two years old) in warm thin layers with a hat and, because they cannot clearly communicate their discomfort verbally, look often for signs of cold or overheating. Feel their extremities—ears, nose, fingers, and toes. Fleece bunting bags are ideal.

Three- to Six-Year-Olds

Little kids may be so busy playing that their sensations go unnoticed. They need a wicking layer and clothing that is easily put on and taken off. Jackets and pants should be sized to provide growing room with no loss of insulation.

Kids over Six Years Old

Kids need a wicking layer along with insulation and a shell that they can easily manipulate as temperatures and exertion vary. Do not let a child's enthusiasm exceed his common sense. Children often want to keep on playing rather than come indoors just because they are cold.

Older Kids

Older kids want the function and style of adult gear. They are able to use technical features. They're old enough to understand the potential warning signs and dangers of cold and can easily use a layering system.

Protect the Extremities

Over half the body heat a child produces can be lost through the head. In cold or wet weather, always cover a young child's head and neck with a hat or insulating hood. Protect their faces with scarves, balaclavas, and neck gaiters in windy weather. Gloves can be worn under mittens. Two pairs of socks add warmth (make sure shoes or boots are sized to accommodate them).

A Child's Travel Wardrobe

This wardrobe will do for children of all ages. Note additions for infants.

Minimalist
Layer 1: Underlayer

- [ ] 3 T-shirts (1 extra large for pool or beach cover-up)
- [ ] 5 to 8 pairs of underpants (or get Coolmax; you'll need fewer)
- [ ] 1 pair of tights or leggings
- [ ] 1 swimsuit
- [ ] 1 pair of pajamas—a fleece-type blanket sleeper replaces blankets

For babies, add

- [ ] 1 or 2 sleepers
- [ ] 2 onesies (T-shirts that snap at the crotch)

Layer 2: Clothing

- [ ] 2 long-sleeved shirts (1 light)
- [ ] 2 or 3 long pants or overalls (1 can be sweatpants if cool weather is expected)
- [ ] 2 pairs of shorts or skirts (or 1 of each)
- [ ] 1 sweatshirt with a hood or a thin, warm sweater
- [ ] 1 nice outfit, if needed

Layer 3: Outerlayer

- [ ] packable rainjacket with hood

Layer 4: Extremities

- [ ] 5 pairs of socks or 2 pairs of infant booties

- [ ] 1 pair of sneakers (black will serve as "dressy" in many restaurants)
- [ ] 1 pair of active sandals
- [ ] 1 pair of dress shoes, if needed
- [ ] sun hat with a wide brim and a means of tying it in the wind (chin tie, elasticized headband); ear and neck flaps are good too—try those made by Flap Happy

For cold-weather travel, add

- [ ] silk- or polyester-knit long underwear, top and bottom (for cold weather)
- [ ] 3 pairs of thin socks for sock liners
- [ ] a fleece baby bag, vest, or jacket
- [ ] an appropriate outer shell
- [ ] glove liners, mittens
- [ ] a wool or fleece hat, with ear flaps

Special Accessories for Kids

These items will make a child's journey smoother and more comfortable.

Children's EarPlanes
These disposable earplug-like devices are for children ages five to twelve who suffer from ear discomfort during takeoff and landing, either due to cold, allergies, and sinus conditions, or just "because." An adult version is also available for ages twelve and up.

Travel Washcloths (Microfiber) or Handiwipes
Packtowls are invaluable for sponging, mopping, wiping, and so on. Buy at least one, cut one-third of it into small washcloths, and use the other two-thirds as a towel or mop-up cloth.

Travel Pillow
You can find baby-sized travel pillows.

Nightlight

Do not forget one of these for unfamiliar hotel rooms. Buy one abroad for 220-volt use. Lightsticks are a good alternative.

Equipment for Babies and Small Children

To go carry-on, you can take at most a car seat and/or (depending on the airline) a portable umbrella stroller or a child-carrier onto the plane. Arrange, rent, or borrow cribs and other equipment in advance.

Turbulence Protection

An infant or toddler on your lap in the airplane is vulnerable to injury from turbulence. To prevent this, you can buy a turbulence protection vest. The vest is worn by the child, and a tether on the vest back loops around the parent's regular lap safety belt.

The vest comes in two sizes for infants and toddlers.

Car Seat

If you will be driving or flying with a ticketed child, you will need an FAA-approved car seat (they are labeled accordingly). This will also provide a comfortable place for the baby to eat and sleep. Some car rental agencies rent car seats. If the flight is not full (call ahead), it pays to bring the car seat with you to the gate. If there is room, they will seat you next to an empty seat; if the plane is full, the crew will stow or check the car seat. You can always ask them to keep it inside the cabin; they may oblige.

Sit'n'Stroll

Finally, a combination stroller/car seat! This is a collapsible stroller with a removable car seat that is comfortable enough for the baby to be in at home or while traveling.

NOTE: The stroller must be checked through, as it is oversize.

Umbrella Stroller

If you will be driving and your sightseeing stops are accessible to strollers (some museums do not allow them), take a compact umbrella stroller with small, sturdy, easily maneuvered double wheels. Make sure that it collapses easily and can be carried with one hand.

Backpack Child Carriers

Carrying a child on your back is ideal if you will be taking public transportation, hiking, or walking on terrain where strollers are not convenient. Backpack carriers also provide freer access for the parent maneuvering in crowds, stores, and other public places. A small child can remain in a backpack carrier all day, resting, sightseeing, and sleeping at will. Tough Traveler manufactures frame child carriers for kids between the ages of six months (when they can sit up with their heads unsupported) and four years. These carriers collapse and are easily stowed in the overhead bin. Kelty also makes a good line of child carriers.

When choosing a child carrier, consider its primary use and your comfort as well as baby's. If the pack will be baby's sole mode of transportation with lots of all-day hiking and walking (and baby sleeping), Tough Traveler's highly technical Kid Carrier will be most comfortable for parent and child. It takes loads of up to fifty pounds and fits parents between five feet, one inch and six feet, four inches tall. The carrier has fully padded straps and waistbands, back ventilation, and lots of control straps to distribute the load. The even more elaborate Filly ensures long-range comfort (all-day and longer hiking) when carrying loads of up to sixty pounds. This one is appropriate for giving older kids a respite. For a simpler, less expensive pack that's ideal for local trips and short hikes, the Montana still offers parents control straps and a sternum (chest) strap to distribute the load.

All packs have a large pouch under the seat for storing diapers, gear, and snacks. Optional equipment includes a rain or sun hood, stirrups, and, on the Kid Carrier, a side pocket set.

Take a small pocket mirror along so that you can see your child and make sure she's wearing her hat.

Soft Carriers for Infants

Soft infant carriers are convenient for holding infants between birth and nine months of age against the parent's body in a hands-free mode. Easily stowed, they are ideal for travel. Choose one that supports the baby's head and allows baby to see out. A quick-drying fabric is an advantage.

A Place to Sleep

Portable cribs have no place as carry-on luggage; consider other sleeping arrangements or rent beds at your destination.

Here are some ideas for baby's sleep arrangements:

- Use your blanket to line a drawer for baby to sleep in.

- Make a small bedroll: Cut a piece of Insulite bought at a camping store and cover it with a rubberized protector pad and a small sheet. Roll and strap it to the bottom of your travel pack.

- Lullaby Lane website (www.lullabylane.com) offers the Dex Porta Bed Genie 3 In 1. You can take this all-in-one diaper bag, changing table, and bed anywhere!

Diapers

If you will be traveling where baby supplies are available, pack light. Bring enough trim, extra-absorbent diapers to get you to your destination. Be open-minded about other brands. If you are going off the beaten path, take cloth diapers and wraps that you can wash and reuse (see *Adventuring with Children* by Nan Jeffrey, Foghorn Press, 1992). Pack a few extra diapers for emergencies.

10

PACKING FOR TEENS

Why a separate chapter for teenagers? There are two reasons. One, teens are very fashion conscious and tend to overpack. Two, they underestimate the necessity of protecting their valuables.

Experienced teen travelers know that traveling light is the way to go. Forget that big suitcase! Get a convertible backpack with a detachable daypack (see pp. 19–20), use the Bundle Method outlined in chapter 6, and you will be set to go to camp, Europe, or any study program for weeks or months.

If you love fashion, here is your challenge: create the greatest number of outfits possible from the fewest pieces of clothing, using layering principles along the way. Start early and refine your wardrobe before the trip. Then pack it and walk a mile carrying it. If you cannot handle it easily, go home and start throwing items out.

Follow the wardrobe guidelines outlined in earlier chapters. Here are the key points: If traveling abroad, choose clothing that is appropriate, in terms of culture and climate, for your destination. Ask your sponsoring hosts or others who have been there. Shorts, revealing clothing, and sports clothing, for example, are not acceptable in many locales. Skirts may be more appropriate than slacks would be. One-piece swimsuits may be more acceptable than bikinis. If you are visiting religious sites, take a scarf to cover your head and shoulders. You can check out trendy but modest (higher neckline) camisoles at the website www.coverwear.com.

Coordinate your clothing around a two-color scheme. Add a third or fourth color for accents. If all your items are interchangeable, you can create a wide variety of outfits. Separates will add flexibility. Choose loose, comfortable clothing that will accommodate a security wallet.

If you will be hand washing, leave your jeans at home or take two pairs. They are hard to wash by hand and dry very slowly.

All items of clothing should function as part of a layering system. Instead of a few bulky items, pack several thin layers, including insulating underwear, short- and long-sleeved shirts, a sweater, and outerwear.

Use accessories to add variety. Colorful belts, hair decorations, hose, and socks do not weigh much. Unless you are traveling where none will be available, take only what makeup and toiletries you need. Use sample sizes or decant products into small plastic bottles. Remember that you have only two clothing colors so you do not need a variety of makeup colors. If you will be gone a long time, have Mom or Dad ship you some of your favorite shampoo midway through the trip.

The following wardrobe list is based on the one recommended by the Council on International Educational Exchange (CIEE) in its book *Going Places: The High School Student's Guide to Study, Travel, and Adventure Abroad* (St. Martin's Press, 1993). Also refer to the Basic Adventure Wardrobe lists in chapter 8. This wardrobe will fit into a convertible pack and suffice for short or long, spring and summer trips. Remember, the less you pack, the more room you have for things you'll buy on your trip!

Travel Wardrobe for Teens

For short trips, pack the minimum number of items recommended. Adjust the mixture of slacks, skirts, and shorts depending on your personal style, the cultural customs of your destination, and your planned activities. Choose light and medium weights in easy-care fabrics. Pack a sweater in an accessible place.

Clothes

In your main bag, pack the following.

Layer 1: Underlayer

NOTE: All items should be moisture wicking and quick drying.

- [ ] 2 camisoles or tank tops to go with skirts as well as pants (for boys, polo-type shirts are more versatile)

- [ ] 1 extra-large T-shirt (beach cover-up, nightshirt)

- [ ] 1 pair of leggings or tights to sleep in or for extra warmth

- [ ] 4 to 7 pairs of underpants (3 if you buy Coolmax)

- [ ] 7 pairs of socks (3 if you buy Coolmax)

- [ ] 1 or 2 pairs of hose or tights, if needed (more if you wear an odd size)

- [ ] 2 or 3 bras

- [ ] 1 swimsuit

Layer 2: Clothing

- [ ] 2 pairs of long pants

- [ ] 1 or 2 skirts

- [ ] 1 short-sleeved blouse or shirt

- [ ] 1 or 2 long-sleeved shirts (1 light for sun protection, 1 heavier)

- [ ] 1 pair of shorts (knee length)

- [ ] 1 or 2 sweaters or jackets (1 nice, thin warm sweater, and 1 sweatshirt or a casual jacket)

- [ ] 1 dressy outfit in packable fabric, if needed

- [ ] sports clothing as needed

Layer 3: Outerwear

- ☐ 1 rainjacket with hood
- ☐ 1 travel umbrella

Layer 4: Extremities

- ☐ 1 pair of sneakers or walking shoes
- ☐ 1 pair of sandals or flip-flops
- ☐ 1 pair of dress shoes
- ☐ 1 or 2 belts
- ☐ 1 small, packable purse
- ☐ bandannas, scarves
- ☐ cap or packable sun hat
- ☐ tie, hair accessories, jewelry (not valuable)

Gear for Teens

Also in your main bag, pack the following, not all of which you may need (see chapter 3 for details):

- ☐ toiletry kit (with small and sample-sized containers)
- ☐ small dual-voltage travel steamer, iron, or hairdryer with appropriate adapter plugs (try to avoid this sort of equipment)
- ☐ travel towel and washcloth
- ☐ some resealable plastic bags (sandwich and gallon size)
- ☐ travel alarm clock
- ☐ flashlight and extra batteries
- ☐ first-aid kit
- ☐ sewing kit
- ☐ laundry kit
- ☐ eating utensils (cup, spoon, fork, plastic plate)

- [ ] pictures of your family and home to show new friends
- [ ] guidebooks and maps or photocopied pages in manila envelopes
- [ ] fold-up, expandable, nylon tote bag
- [ ] inflatable pillow and ear plugs for noisy hotels
- [ ] small gifts for your hosts

In your daypack or tote bag, pack

- [ ] eyeglasses and sunglasses with retainer
- [ ] contact lens and supplies
- [ ] orthodontic appliances and case
- [ ] prescription medication and folding cup
- [ ] sunscreen, lip balm
- [ ] cosmetic kit (keep it small!)
- [ ] water bottle, snack
- [ ] pocket knife (cannot be brought on the plane; buy there)
- [ ] journal or diary, pens, postcards, stationery
- [ ] small camera and film or smart media, batteries
- [ ] personal MP3 player/iPod, headphones
- [ ] book, games, cards
- [ ] current map, guidebook, brochures

Security for Teens

Some teens think of a money belt as an unnecessary hassle that will spoil their outfits. They also feel immune from theft of important items such as a passport, their traveler's checks, cash, credit cards, phone card, airline tickets, student ID, and so on.

Chances are, nothing will happen. But don't tempt people who are in the business of stealing from unsuspecting travelers. You don't need to be paranoid; just be smart and take responsibility for your personal and material safety. Keep your valuables in a security wallet and wear it *at all times* when you are traveling around, sleeping on the train, or staying in a hostel. Do not leave anything valuable in your luggage or daypack. Wear the security wallet hidden *under your clothing*, not hanging around your neck outside your shirt—this is an open invitation to thieves. (I don't even like the neck strap to show under my shirt.)

Luckily, hassle-free security wallets are comfortable and their contents accessible. This vertical pouch has an adjustable strap that you can wear in a variety of ways. The best way to wear it is around your waist, tucked down inside your slacks, skirt, or shorts like a hanging pocket. It is easy to pull in and out, and you don't have to wear a belt. If you are wearing tight pants or skirt (clothes are more comfortable when they are loose-fitting, by the way), the wallet can also be worn around the neck under your shirt (do not let the neck straps show). Or you can shorten the cord and wear the pouch underneath your arm like a holster, or lengthen it and wear it diagonally across your chest, with the pouch tucked into your pants or skirt.

The pouch has three pockets: one long, zippered compartment for traveler's checks, tickets, documents, cash, and so on; an open pocket for your passport and passes; and a third, small zippered pocket on the flap for credit cards and a bit of cash or change. I really like this small pocket: when the pouch is tucked in, you can lift out the flap to have quick access to tip money without having to pull out the whole wallet. For more on security, see the following chapter.

If you develop the skills of packing right and protecting yourself now, you will be prepared to become a real *traveler*—not just a tourist—mobile enough to wander the world, meet wonderful people, and see wonderful places.

11

SECURITY

A s a carry-on traveler, you avoid the risk of lost and pilfered luggage. Here are some other precautions you can take to protect yourself and your belongings. For a complete discussion of security and contingency planning, read *The Safe Travel Book* by Peter Savage (Macmillan, 1993). Many of the tips mentioned here come from his book.

Protecting Travel Documents and Valuables

Wear a security wallet *at all times*, whether you are awake or asleep, and hide any visible straps. My two favorites are the adjustable World Class Passport Carrier from Easy Going, and the Eagle Creek Undercover Security Wallet. The World Class Passport Carrier has a steel cable running through the straps so that it cannot be cut off. The Undercover Security Wallet is a lighter weight, versatile money pouch. Many other types are available. See pages 45–48 for a full discussion.

Always carry your passport, cash, half of your traveler's checks, your credit cards, address and phone list, and copies of prescriptions in that security wallet. Do not be tempted to pack them anywhere else. To split your risk, carry the remaining half of your traveler's checks in your luggage. Pack your traveler's check record separately from your checks. Keep only a small amount of cash in your wallet or a sturdy nylon pouch you use as a wallet. See pages 48–49 for a list of valuables.

Give a home contact copies of all your documents, including the first page of your passport, credit-card account numbers, redemption-center phone numbers, and itinerary. This person can cancel your credit cards if they are lost or stolen and send you copies overnight of anything you need quickly.

When making long-distance calls, hide the keypad or use an automatic phone dialer or swipe-through credit card to protect against theft of your account number.

You may store valuables in the hotel safe-deposit box if you feel that the hotel security is untrustworthy. Make sure the safe's contents are covered by the hotel's insurance policy. Get a signed, itemized receipt for the items stored.

If you must store valuables in your room, use a Pac-Safe Travel Safe. You can secure it to a fixed piece of furniture (see chapter 3). Or hide your valuables. You can buy hide-a-safes of various sorts or make a safe by cutting the inner pages out of a paperback book. But the best strategy of all is to travel without those valuables that you can't easily carry with you at all times.

At the beach, put your valuables in a Seal Pack or other watertight security wallet (see p. 48) that you can wear while swimming.

As much as possible, use traveler's checks and credit cards instead of cash.

For incidental expenses, carry only a little cash in local currency or small U.S. bills in your day bag, purse, front pocket, fanny pack, or wallet in a front pocket or an inside jacket pocket. Everything else should be in your security wallet at all times.

Do not put valuables in a purse, and if someone tugs at your purse, let it go.

Do not wear expensive-looking jewelry and watches. They attract attention.

Include the following phone numbers on your address list, carried in your security wallet:

- [ ] your contact person at home who has copies of all documents

- [ ] the U.S. embassy and the twenty-four-hour telephone number of the U.S. mission. These numbers are available from the State Department in Washington, D.C., online.

- [ ] numbers for reporting lost or stolen credit cards and contacting traveler's check centers (including any after-hours number)

- [ ] your travel agent's twenty-four-hour number, if any

- [ ] your emergency medical insurance company's twenty-four-hour assistance number or the number of an English-speaking doctor (see Travel Medicine in appendix 2, Resources)

- [ ] your automobile insurance company's emergency assistance number

- [ ] your long-distance calling-card assistance number as well as any additional country codes you may need. When using the telephone, memorize your card code and shield your fingers when inputting your card number (a common scam is for thieves at the airport to steal your card number by watching you punch your number in), or use phones that allow you to slide the card through.

- [ ] your physician and lawyer contact numbers

Leave at home important items that you are unlikely to need while traveling, such as social security and local credit cards.

Luggage

Do not use expensive-looking luggage. It attracts attention. Label each piece of luggage inside and out with your name and business address or your next destination. Be sure your luggage is locked. If you check luggage through, watch to make sure it is tagged and routed properly. Attach a luggage strap, colored yarn, or tape to help you identify your bag when you retrieve it. Many bags look alike these days.

At the airport, thieves steal bags, laptops, cell phones, and the like off the X-ray machine's conveyor belt while the owner is walking through the metal detector. Make sure that you can go through the detector quickly by putting all metal items, such as large belt buckles, keys, and anything else that might set off the metal detector, inside your carry-on in advance. Then, after putting your luggage on the conveyor, do not take your eyes off it. If you are traveling with a companion, take turns going through the detector and watching your luggage.

While waiting, keep your luggage between your ankles. Consider using a retractable cable lock to fasten luggage to a bench or fence if you will be waiting long.

Keep any valuables, such as a camera, computer, jewelry, and so on, locked in your daypack or tote bag. Or ship them ahead. Most airlines exclude these from liability coverage in checked luggage.

If you want to take a short day trip, check your luggage and equipment at the train station or a hotel.

In many places, daypacks and purses are commonly slashed and items are stolen without you even noticing. To prevent losing your belongings, you can line the sides and bottoms of your bag or fanny pack with gutter screen to be found at the hardware store. Or check out the daypacks, pack covers, and other products lined with eXomesh by Pac-Safe.

Medicine

Never put your medication in checked luggage. Always carry it with you. Divide your medication into two containers. If one is lost, you'll have a backup. If you are traveling with another person, be sure that they know exactly where your medication is stored. Carry prescription copies along with the phone number of your doctor and pharmacy in your security wallet. Leave a copy of this information at home with someone you can easily reach because it is not always possible to fill prescriptions in foreign destinations.

Personal Security

Maintain heightened awareness at all times; this is your best protection.

In Your Hotel

- Be alert when checking in and out of a hotel; do not flash your cash around.

- Learn the location of hotel exits.

- Book a room near a busy area or an elevator.

- Make sure your room has a peephole and double dead bolt locks. You can pack a portable lock (see appendix 2, Resources), such as PortaBolt.

- Call the front desk to verify unexpected deliveries.

- Small hotels are generally safer than large facilities. Strangers are instantly noticed.

- Small intruder alarms and smoke alarms are available. Consider these.

- If brown-outs will be a possibility, carry neon-like lightsticks to use as night lights. They are available at camping-supply stores.

Around Town

- Do not look vulnerable or lost. Walk with a purpose and stay alert to what's happening around you.

- Ask the hotel about the safety of a neighborhood and about areas to be avoided. Ask whether it is safe to walk alone.

- Before taking a cab, ask the concierge for directions and costs.

- Conventioneers: if you are attending a convention, obtain advance information about the city (maps and guides will be your best source) and, when there, remove your name tag when you are out of the convention area.

In Your Rental Car

- Have keys in hand when you approach the car. Look in, around, and under the car before getting in.

- Plan your route before you leave. Tourists stopped at a traffic light and looking at a map are targets for theft and carjackings.

- Keep your car in gear when stopped at a light.

- Ask directions from officials.

- Never leave valuables in your car. Unpack at your hotel when you reach your destination, and make sure that you don't leave cameras, money, passports, laptops, cell phone, business papers, keys, or anything that is important to you in your vehicle. If you are stopping off at a museum or dinner along the way, try to park in a guarded lot. If you can't do so, try to have your valuables in a locked single bag that you can carry with you to the restaurant or check at the museum coatroom. If you're traveling by car ferry, don't leave valuables in your vehicle.

- Check your auto insurance before you leave home. It may not cover you for car rentals abroad. If this is the case, buying insurance with your car rental is a good idea.

When it comes to security and theft problems, most trips are uneventful. Just exercise the same precautions that you do at home, and you are bound to have a safe and enjoyable trip.

12

PACKING FOR THE
JOURNEY HOME

By the end of your trip, your clothes are dirty, you're tired, and you just don't care anymore. Am I right? But congratulations—you did it!!

Here are some packing tips for going home.

Check Your List

As you pack, use your packing list to make sure you didn't forget anything. Keep your list with you. You can review it on the plane coming home, noting things you didn't need and items you wished you had packed. You will also need it for insurance claim purposes should your check-through luggage get lost.

Laundry

Dirty laundry: when your soiled garments are voluminous, your clean bundle is spare. Make a bundle of your clean duds if you're not wearing them, then lay your dirty laundry on top (you can put it in a stuff sack or plastic bag), or place laundry in a separate compartment. Or put it in your last-minute bag and carry it to the laundromat or all the way home.

Pack It In, Pack It Out

Pack the bundle going home the same way you did to leave. I packed for my editor for a European business trip (he's six-foot-something and had suits), and he couldn't believe that I fit everything into a carry-on. When he got back he said he tried to just stuff it all back in and got nowhere fast! Luckily he remembered the Bundle Method, and he was able to come home without buying another suitcase. By the end of your trip, you will be a pro at using the Bundle Method! However, many of us buy more clothes or other items on the trip—that's a good reason to stow a fold-up nylon bag, just in case.

Packing Shortcut

If you are concerned that the U.S. Customs will inspect the contents of your suitcase, use the following Quick-Fix Bundle Method before coming home. It will decrease the time it takes to repack at customs.

1. Lay all your garments in the bag, stacking the collars in one direction.

2. Drape the sleeves out.

3. Drape the bottoms out.

4. Put in your core pouch.

5. To close the bundle, bring all the left sleeves in, then all the right sleeves, then the hems.

Voilà! There is your bundle. Now, if they ask to look inside your suitcase, let them! It is easy to unfurl and close up again. But don't tempt customs. Have all your paperwork and declarable items ready and waiting to be inspected.

Dealing with Accumulation

What do you do with all of your guidebook pages, maps, tourist brochures, souvenir admissions tickets, and other sundry items you gather along the way? What about purchases? What about film? How do you avoid dragging it all with you?

You can pack a fold-up nylon suitcase, such as the last-minute bag, to carry home souvenirs.

You can accept the fact that you can't resist shopping and bring (or buy) a big suitcase, and be prepared to pay the price!

Or you can use one of the following methods.

Buy Compact Souvenirs

Buy small, compact things instead of big, heavy ones. Items like scarves, jewelry, T-shirts, and fabric are suitable choices. Or make collections of fun, cheap, easily found items such as postcards, patches, paper money, and so on. You can pack flat items such as small prints in manila folders and store them in flat pockets or underneath your bundle on the divider. Avoid breakables. However, you can pack small breakables in the middle of your bundle, and they will be well cushioned. Or wrap them in a Packtowl or bubble wrap and keep them in your daypack.

Mail Packages Home

Shipping merchandise is the best thing you can do for large and bulky items, even if it is costly. Make shipping a part of your trip budget. This can be a complicated procedure, depending on the country. Only ship from reliable merchants. Otherwise, ship it yourself from a post office. Try to plan your mailing points in advance. Find out as much as you can from other travelers and guidebook information. You may have to devote a lot of time to going to the post office, finding out the rules, and going out to buy paper, string, tape, and other supplies.

Always carry a permanent marker with you for labeling packages. Put the destination inside the package as well as on the outside. Declare what is inside (be circumspect—specific details are unnecessary). Always watch the complete transaction, then hope for the best. Notify the recipient by separate letter that the package is arriving, and list what is in it so they can check whether anything is missing.

Paper-based items you want to have on your trip—such as brochures, used maps, guidebooks and photocopied guidebook pages, book admissions tickets, and so on—can be packed in 10 x 13-inch manila envelopes labeled with their subject country. When you are done with them, mail them home to yourself.

Carry film home in clear zip-locking bags, or have it developed and mail the prints home. You can also buy prepaid film-processor mailing envelopes from your local dealer before you go, though from some countries this can be risky. Address them to your home or business.

CUSTOMS NOTE: You are allowed to mail home goods worth up to $200 of your $400 exemption, provided they are labeled for your personal use and you do not exceed one addressee per day. Used clothing that you brought with you can be shipped home; if it has not been altered, it is exempt. Label the box "American Goods Returned." Bona fide gifts of not more than $50 in fair retail value can be received by friends and relatives in the United States free of duty and tax, if the same person does not receive more than $50 in gift shipments in one day. Perfumes valued at more than $5 retail, tobacco products, and alcoholic beverages are excluded from the gift provision. Gifts for more than one person may be consolidated in the same package provided they are individually wrapped and labeled with the name of the recipient. Mark the outer wrapping of each package "unsolicited gift" and indicate the nature of gift and its fair retail value. Mark the box "consolidated gifts" with the names of the recipients listed and the value of each gift. This will facilitate customs clearance of your package.

VAT Exemptions

When you purchase goods in foreign countries, a 15 to 20 percent Value Added Tax (VAT) is paid at point of purchase for many items. Ask for a special VAT exempt invoice when you pay for an item. Keep these VAT receipts with your important documents. Upon leaving the foreign country, you can submit these receipts to the customs agent and the sales tax will be reimbursed to you via mail. Or a voucher may be given to you that you can redeem at a bank in the airport before you leave. Some quick research in a guidebook or a question to your travel agent will help you know what to expect.

Customs Guidelines

1. All travelers are allowed a $400 exemption based on the fair retail value of each item in the country where acquired if one of the following applies:

    - The items are for personal or household use.

    - You bring the items with you at the time of return to the United States, and they are properly declared at customs (articles purchased and left for alterations or other reasons cannot be applied to your $400 exemption when shipped to follow at a later date—duty is assessed when received).

    - You've been gone at least forty-eight hours (does not apply for Mexico and the U.S. Virgin Islands).

    - You have not used this $400 exemption or any part of it within the preceding thirty-day period.

    - A joint declaration for a family returning as a unit can be made, with an exemption of $400 for each person regardless of age. Family members making joint declarations may combine their personal exemptions, even if the articles acquired by one member of the family exceed the personal exemption allowed.

- Cigarettes, cigars, and liquor have separate requirements. Travelers returning from Insular U.S. possessions have different rules. For complete information, contact the U.S. Customs Service. They offer a pamphlet and a website; see the Travel tab, especially the "When You Return to the United States" page at www.cbp.gov/xp/cgov/travel/vacation/kbyg/return_to_us.xml.

2. Returning U.S. residents and nonresidents must declare the following:

   - Articles that you purchased
   - Gifts presented to you while abroad, such as wedding or birthday gifts
   - Articles purchased in duty-free shops
   - Repairs or alterations made to any articles taken abroad and returned, whether or not repairs or alterations were free of charge
   - Items you have been requested to bring home for another person
   - Any articles you intend to sell or use in your business

3. U.S. Customs warns that if you understate the value of an article you declare, or if you otherwise misrepresent an article in your declaration, you may have to pay a penalty in addition to payment of duty. Under certain circumstances, the article could be seized and forfeited if the penalty is not paid.

4. On the way home, keep your purchases together and your receipts with you in a plastic bag or manila envelope. Have them readily available so that you can fill out the declaration forms on the plane and so customs can examine them easily. In most cases, the inspection will be perfunctory. Fill out only the identification portion of the declaration form on the plane. Then you can orally declare your purchases if they fall within

the $400 exemption. If you know you have more than this, fill out the entire form with a complete list of merchandise.

Damaged Luggage

1. Check all baggage for damage before leaving the airport. Once you're out the door, it's often too late. Typically, retailers and manufacturers do not cover air-carrier damage.

2. Find out the airline's damage liability for baggage. Each allows a certain dollar amount loss per passenger.

3. Damage liability rarely covers loss of valuables, jewelry, cameras, computers, and the like.

4. In case of luggage loss, your packing list will come in very handy when you fill out your claim form. Also, any receipts you have will be helpful.

A1

THE TOP TEN CARRY-ON
PACKING TIPS

1. Resolve that you want to travel light.

2. Buy the right luggage. Limit yourself to one main 22-inch bag and one smaller tote-size bag.

3. Make a packing list. When in doubt, leave it out!

4. Choose a color scheme and stick to it.

5. When selecting clothes, pack thin layers for changing temperatures. Know the attributes of various fabrics. Choose simply styled coordinates in maintainable fabrics.

6. For gear, make small kits. Pack toiletries, medical kit, and laundry and office supplies in pouches. Use small plastic bottles and sample sizes.

7. Pack money and documents in a security wallet. Wear it on your body underneath your clothing, even for short trips.

8. Don't forget your photo ID or passport—you can't even board the plane without these!

9. Mail home paper, souvenirs, purchases, and such as you travel.

10. After your trip, review your packing list. Cross out what you didn't need and write down what you wish you had brought. Save this list —it will be like gold when it's time to pack again!

A2

RESOURCES

It is amazing how many resources are now available for the traveler. Many luggage, gear, and clothing manufacturers offer catalogs with detailed descriptions of their wares both in paper and on the Internet. You can easily surf the Web to peruse the goods and be referred to a retailer where you can actually go and see the merchandise. Or you can call and request a product catalog or find out where to go locally to shop. Some companies also take orders directly from consumers.

In addition to looking in traditional luggage stores and mail-order catalogs, make sure to locate the specialty travel store in your area. These eclectic shops conveniently offer a broad selection of travel books, maps, luggage, travel gear, and sometimes travel clothing. The staff is always knowledgeable, and the merchandise is hand-selected by owner and staff.

The following are my some of my favorite websites.

Luggage and Travel Gear

Easy Going Travel Shop and Bookstore
www.easygoing.com (online catalog sales)
(800) 675-5500
email: info@easygoing.com

Easy Going is close to my heart because I helped open it in 1979 and worked in it during much of the 1980s. It is a tremendous resource to travelers, and the staff is very knowledgeable.

Although the retail stores have closed, www.easygoing.com is still a great website for many of your travel needs. They have an ever-changing array of quality, useful travel luggage and gear.

Many of the items mentioned in this book (and more) are available at www.easygoing.com. They sell carry-on and checkable luggage (Easy Going Special Edition Three-Compartment Carry-on Bag; Eagle Creek Cargo Switchback; Travelpro, Kiva, Delsey, and Rick Steves packs and wheelaboards); organizing aids (including the recommended core pouch Carry-Rite Mini-Organizer, Eagle Creek Pack-It system, and zippered nylon organizer pouches); Last-Minute expandable nylon fold-up tote bags; security wallets (including the World Class Passport Carrier, Undercover Security Wallet, and others); Flexo-line; travel towels; luggage locks; dual-voltage travel appliances; converters, transformers, and electrical adapters; phone-jack adapters; travel soap and spot removers; No-Jet-Lag, EarPlanes, and Sea Band; and Pac-Safe security products. They have a secured website catalog, and they welcome phone inquiries and mail orders.

Smart Luggage

Ameribag
www.ameribag.com
(800) 246-1292
The original Healthy Back Bag—a tote bag with ergonomic weight distribution. Sold at many travel, luggage, and outdoor stores.

Atlantic Luggage Company
www.atlanticluggage.com
(888) 8-ATLANTIC
Atlantic has a unique QUAD-WHEEL design in which two extra wheels pop out for stability and stress relief for your back.

Carry-rite of California
www.carryrite.com
(800) 321-6113

Manufacturer of the Mini 5-Pocket Organizer (#315), which I use for the core pouch. They will refer you to a dealer in your area.

Delsey Luggage
(410) 796-5655
www.delsey.com

Delsey makes the Helium line of luggage, which, as its name suggests, is quite lightweight. Their retractable handle casing is a bit bigger than ideal, but otherwise it is a quality line in a good price range.

Eagle Creek Travel Gear
www.eaglecreek.com
(800) 874-1048

Eagle Creek products are ubiquitous in outdoor, luggage, and travel stores. Their ever-widening line of merchandise includes hybrid travelpack/wheelaboards, conventional packs and wheelaboards, travel gear, the relatively new Pack-It packing system, and the Continental Journey Women's Fit travelpack and a diaper-bag daypack.

KIVA
www.kivadesigns.com
(707) 748-1614

A really nice line of luggage in a good price range.

MEI Travel Packs, by Genuine Gear
www.meipacks.com
(559) 266-0192
Also available at www.lahostels.org

MEI currently has limited distribution and a website in progress as of this publication. They are the original convertible travel-pack company, and their designs and quality are beautiful in their simplicity. Call the manufacturer for a catalog. I recommend the

Flying Scotsman I and the Trekker I for carry-on size. These are internal frame packs with hip belts and lumbar support. The Trekker is a little more technical than the Scotsman. For casual use, the Convertible is the good pack for packing under 20 pounds. It has no hip belt.

Tough Traveler
www.toughtraveler.com
(800) 468-6844

Tough Traveler makes the Super Padre travelpack, which ergonomically fits to your body. It is unique in that they make several for people of all sizes, from age 5 to 100.

Tutto Luggage (also called "Healthy Luggage")
www.tutto.com
(877) 608-8886

The unique collapsible luggage with four wheels and a pullbar to prevent stress on the arms and hands. A full line of sizes, plus a kids' carry-on. Also, the wonderful rolling Office on Wheels. This is high-quality luggage—definitely consider it!

Travelpro
www.TravelproUSA.com
(561) 998-2824

The originator of upright wheeled luggage, Travelpro continues to innovate with great designs and quality in every price range. They make a suiter rollaboard. Good features include an ergonomic handle, no-tip foot, and lots of accessory bags that can be hung on the suitcase.

Victorinox (makers of the original Swiss Army Knife)
www.swissarmy.com
(888) 658-0717

As efficient and sleek as the knives they created, this upscale line of luggage and accessories has simple, elegant, yet functional designs. Their carry-on sizes include a wheeled garment bag, a tri-fold garment bag (that can fit under the seat or overhead), a

22-inch Pullman, and the hybrid wheeled travelpack Trek Pack Series. Their Nth Series are even more technical packs. Also a broad range of accessories bags and gear.

Specialty Travel Gear

Campmor
www.campmor.com
(800) 226-7667
Their online and print catalogs offer a wide range of equipment for the traveler and outdoor enthusiast.

Magellan's
www.magellans.com
(800) 962-4943
Their well-known online and print catalogs are stocked with lots of travel gear, including mobile computing equipment.

Here are other specialty travel supplies websites I like:

- www.LeTravelStore.com: also a retail location in San Diego, California

- www.christinecolumbus.com: features half-slip with pockets and other merchandise geared toward the woman traveler

- www.onebag.com: a great travel site website by Dick Dymant

- www.ProTravelGear.com: seems to be oriented toward pilots

- www.ricksteves.com

- www.travelproducts.com

Walkabout Travel Gear
www.walkabouttravelgear.com
(800) 852-7085
Lots of great travel items and luggage in this paper and online catalog. Also lots of information on mobile computing and electricity needs.

Mobile Computing Gear

Obviously, if you need this information you are a savvy internet researcher. However, here are some websites that are reliable for understanding the ins and outs of globetrotting with your computer:

- www.easygoing.com

- www.gomobile.com

- www.teleadapt.com

- www.walkabouttravelgear.com

- www.laptoptravel.com

- www.pcworld.com: Lots of articles on all sorts of aspects of mobile travel

- www.seatguru.com: Tells you if your airplane has access to power for your computer

Computer and Camera Bags

Most of the previously listed luggage manufacturers also make briefcase/computer-type bags. The following are specialists in the field and offer very high-quality, innovative designs.

Lowepro USA
www.lowepro.com
(707) 575-4363
Excellent camera totes and luggage sold through retailers.

Tenba Gear
www.tenbagear.com
(914) 347-3300

Tamrac
www.tamrac.com
(800) 662-0717

Specialty Travel Clothing

The following merchants are my favorite vendors of high-quality clothing appropriate for travel. Also check out department stores such as Nordstrom, Bloomingdale's, Talbots, Target, Sears, and Macy's for lots of travel-worthy conventional clothing. Where noted, other gear and children's clothing are available, too.

Coverwear.com
(800) 675-6582

An interesting website featuring "modest" T-shirts and camisoles for teens and women, including higher-cut tank tops and camisoles and cap-sleeve T-shirts, all long enough to stay tucked into low-rise jeans. Sizes youth to 2x.

Coolmaxclothing.com
(760) 401-7100

This website offers a well-priced line of Coolmax underwear, socks and T-shirts for all sizes. This company is owned by a U.S. Army veteran, and the products are made in the USA.

Chico's
www.chicos.com
(888) 855-4986

Chico's Travel Collection offers no fewer than fifty-four pieces! You can choose a starter wardrobe of five basic black pieces. They suggest wearing any two basics and adding a third novelty piece to add interest and color. Up to size 18, no petite or plus sizes, but amply cut, loose-fitting designs.

Ex Officio
www.exofficio.com
(800) 644-7303

Ex Officio specializes in adventure and travel clothing, featuring technical performance fabrics, ventilating systems, SPF 30+ sun protection, and good looks to boot. Designs include a large variety of shirts, convertible slacks with zip-off legs, technical T-shirts, skirts, and nice layering pieces. They also have a full wardrobe selection featuring BUZZ OFF insect-shield fabric.

Kleinerts Garment Shields
www.kleinertsshields.com
(800) 498-7051
Perspiration-protection T-shirts and removable underarm shields to protect your clothing and cut down on laundry. Also sold at some fabric stores.

L.L.Bean
www.llbean.com
(800) 221-4221
All types of high-quality, casual separates and outerwear. Comfort shoes, outdoor gear, and luggage are also included. Silk and polyester thermal underwear seasonally.

Lands' End
www.landsend.com
(800) 356-4444
Wide selection of high-quality, simply styled, durable, casual separates and comfortable shoes. Travelworthy cotton/polyester business shirts. Silk- and polyester-knit long underwear seasonally. Lots for kids, too. Also their own line of soft luggage.

Norm Thompson
www.normthompson.com
(800) 547-1160
Norm Thompson has an unusual selection of versatile, easy-care, classic styles for men and women. Features National Geographic travel clothing and comfortable shoes.

Orvis
www.orvis.com
(888) 235-9763
Orvis has wrinkle-resistant travel blazers with hidden pockets, as well as other well-crafted travel clothing for men and women.

Patagonia and Patagonia Kids
www.patagonia.com
(800) 638-6464

This catalog features high-performance, functional, and attractive clothing for specific climates and activities. Especially interesting are their "Island Hopper" clothing for tropical weather, modest-length Baggies shorts, Synchilla fleece clothing, and Capilene polyester-knit thermal underwear. Patagonia clothing is also sold through retail dealerships. They sell a fleece jacket made from recycled soda bottles! All their cotton products are from organically grown cotton. Patagonia also features their own luggage line.

RailRiders
www.railriders.com
(800) 437-3794

Railriders offers tough, quick-dry clothing for the outdoors and adventure travel. Multi-Tasker Pants have a streamlined look and lots of pockets.

REI—Recreational Equipment Inc.
www.rei.com
(800) 426-4840
TDD: (800) 443-1988

Catalog and multiple retail locations. This excellent retailer offers all kinds of high-performance outdoor equipment, children's packs and carriers, travel packs, clothing, long underwear, shoes, small eating utensils, and other gear. Check out the convertible slacks— long pants that zip off at the knee to become walking shorts. I like to scout around for tiny gear made for backpacking.

Royal Robbins
www.royalrobbins.com
(800) 587-9044

A great website featuring durable travel and casual clothing in a myriad of wrinkle-resistant, comfortable clothing perfect for hot and tropical climates. Also attractive and functional layering pieces.

They have a store in Berkeley, California, and sell through outdoor stores such as REI.

Sahalie
Sahalie.com
(800) 458-4438
This catalog offers a wide array of performance travel clothing and activewear, from underwear to casual separates to fleece.

Sierra Designs
www.sierradesigns.com
(800) 635-0461
(Mail order and local dealer referral)
I like Sierra Designs clothing, which is mostly outdoor-related wear. They have beautiful quality and an informative website for choosing your technical clothing.

Tilley Endurables
www.tilley.com
(800) 363-8737
With a catalog and stores in Canada, this company offers a variety of travel and adventure clothing, much of it made of their special Adventure Cloth—a cotton/polyester blend that promises easy care and comfort. Coordinated separates allow easy selection of mix-and-match items, and attractive silk-like microfiber clothing works well as packable formalwear. Hats, pants, and shorts are available in a huge selection of sizes for the small, large, and tall person. The famous Tilley Hat comes with a four-page owner's manual and is guaranteed never to wear out. They offer a six-piece mix-and-match wardrobe for men and women.

TravelSmith
www.travelsmith.com
(800) 950-1600
Unique in its variety and depth of travel clothing, this company offers carefully coordinated wardrobes for different types of trips and climates. Particular attention is paid to layering function,

activity, and climate. Technical "adventure" clothing is mixed with a nice offering of casual separates. Each item is described in terms of its layering function, weight, and packability. They have plus and petite sizes, which is always a "plus"!

The Walk Shop
www.walkshop.com
(510) 849-3628

Excellent selection of comfortable shoes. A very knowledgeable staff can help you make the right selection. Website sales and retail store in Berkeley, California.

Weekenders Casuals
www.weekendersusa.com
(847) 465-1666 (for referral to a salesperson in your area)

This high-quality, versatile line of highly packable and easily maintained cotton/polyester knit separates is sold by individual consultants nationally. They have a basic, classic line of nine coordinated pieces (in black, navy, white, and red) available year-round, and a fall/winter and spring/summer line that changes annually based on current designer fashions. Appropriate for travel and work. Their store is located in Chicago, Illinois

Wickers Underwear for Anywhere
www.wickers.com
(800) 648-7024
New York City residents (631) 543-1700

Performance long underwear and layering pieces, underwear, and a nightgown specifically designed for women experiencing night sweats. Most sizes available.

Wintersilks
www.wintersilks.com
(888) 782-2224

Huge year-round selection of silk and silk-blend undergarments, thermal underwear, and clothing for men and women. Nice layering pieces for outdoor and conventional clothing. Plus, petite, and tall sizes too.

The following two catalogs offer a great selection of casual wear, hats, and accessories, all in SPF 30+ fabric, for adults and kids.

Sun Precautions Inc.
www.sunprecautions.com
(800) 882-7860

Sun Clothing, Inc.
www.sunclothing.com
(866) 713-9352

Plus-Size Clothing and Activewear

I especially like these websites (some listed previously) because they offer lots of vacation choices for larger sizes.

Just My Size: www.jms.com (800-261-5902). Lots of great underwear and activewear.

Junonia: www.junonia.com (800-JUNONIA). Activewear for women sizes 14 and up.

TravelSmith: www.travelsmith.com. Plus and petite sizes.

Talbots: www.talbots.com. Plus-size petites as well as regular plus sizes.

Norm Thompson: www.normthompson.com. Many items in larger sizes.

Nordstrom Encore Department: www.nordstrom.com.

Resources for Travel with Kids

www.babiestravellite.com

(888) 450-LITE

Provides worldwide delivery of baby supplies, including diapers, food, bath supplies, breastfeeding equipment, plastic baggies, and cleaning supplies. Order in advance, and it will be at your door when you arrive! They do not rent baby equipment (such as cribs and high chairs) but will refer you to a local business that does in the area you will be staying.

www.flyingwithkids.com

This is an excellent website published by a traveling mom. Specializes in baby travel gear for the plane, with useful links to other resources.

www.familyonboard.com

Supplies and equipment for car, train, and plane travel. They offer Skyway luggage for kids, Strolex Sit 'n' Stroll, kids' travel games, and more.

Kelty

www.kelty.com

(800) 423-2320

Kelty makes a wide range of child carriers and accessories.

Lullaby Lane

www.lullabylane.com

(650) 588-7644

This family-owned business has a great selection of travel equipment in the "Baby on The Go" section of their website, including the Dex combination diaper bag/baby bed. Their store is located in San Mateo, California.

Tough Traveler
www.toughtraveler.com
(800) 468-6844
Children's travel packs, luggage, daypacks, and child-carriers. Sold online and through outdoor retailers. The Super Padre packs are ergonomically correct for all ages! Their store is located in Schenectady, New York.

Tutto Luggage
www.tutto.com
(800) 449-1288
The adorable, brightly colored Kids Carry-on is perfect for the serious child traveler. The 20-inch, four-wheeled underseat suitcase pulls along easily with a U-shaped pullbar and can be used as a seat or loaded with extras.

I also like the following sites for travel planning:

Travel Medicine
www.travmed.com
All about travel health and what you need to be concerned with before you go.

Weather Information
www.wunderground.com—Weather Underground.
Gives weather information, including history of temperature, humidity, rain, and wind chill for each country.

QUESTIONS AND ANSWERS

Here are answers to the questions that I get asked most frequently during my packing classes.

What is the best fabric for travel?
Natural fibers, such as pure cotton and wool, breathe the best, but synthetics, such as polyester, lend wrinkle and stain resistance and dry faster. Wool and wool-blend gabardine are superior for fall, winter, and spring. Cotton and cotton-blend knits are perfect for spring and summer. (See the fabric chart on p. 94 for recommended travel fabrics.)

How many garments can you fit in a suitcase?
Almost every person can pack a basic travel wardrobe (seven to nine pieces) in a carry-on. How much more you can get in will depend on your size and the length and bulk of your garments. Generally, smaller people will be able to pack between ten and sixteen pieces; larger people possibly no more than the minimum seven or eight. Your jacket is the bulkiest item. If you don't pack that, you will have more room for other clothing.

Does this packing system work for larger shoe and clothing sizes?
One of the beauties of the Bundle Method (see chapter 6) is that everyone can use it. The number of items of clothing you can fit

may, however, be limited by your size. People with larger shoes will need to consolidate as much as possible. If both shoes cannot fit along the bottom edge of the bag, you will need to sacrifice other space. The best strategies are to wear one pair and pack one pair or to take a second bag.

What is the rule of thumb about underwear and socks?
It depends on how much you want to wash. To travel extremely light, take two pairs of each in a fabric such as nylon or Coolmax and wash one and wear one. Take eight pairs if you want to wash once a week. I generally take four or five pairs of each. Take an extra pair in cold weather because things dry more slowly then.

How long does it take you to pack?
The hard part of packing is selecting the clothing. Once you have your wardrobe, you will pack clothing in five minutes or less. Replacing accessories takes longer than repacking the clothes.

I tried the Bundle Method, and things still got wrinkled. What am I doing wrong?
Two things could have happened. First, the fabrics you chose may not have traveled well. Second, you may not have packed tightly enough. For the Bundle Method to work, the core and inner items must provide sufficient cushioning and the outer layers must be wrapped tightly around the core. If they are loose or underpacked, more wrinkling will occur.

Do you use plastic dry-cleaning bags and tissue paper?
Plastic dry-cleaning bags are great. The positive side of using plastic is that it reduces friction and allows fabrics to drape naturally, thereby minimizing creasing. Plastic is useful when wrinkle-free appearance is of the highest priority. It is useful in suitcases, suiters, and garment bags in which suits, dresses, and wrinkle-prone blouses and shirts are packed on hangers. You may use it if clothing is folded

in half, such as when it is hung in a garment bag or a wheel-aboard suiter, packed on hangers using the Z-fold method (see p. 138), or folded over in a larger suitcase or duffel bag.

However, if I have a full wardrobe or a casual wardrobe, I do not use plastic for the Bundle Method because the plastic takes up a lot of room in the bag and promotes the shifting of clothing, thereby making it difficult to pack. In hot weather, plastic traps moisture and promotes wrinkling. Also, if you choose fabrics appropriately, you can minimize, if not eliminate, the need for plastic.

I only use tissue paper if I want to cushion a crease. In this case, you can stuff sleeves and put some under collars or other folds.

Do you pack hangers?

I generally pack one small plastic or metal skirt hanger because hotels often don't have them. It goes in my accessory section. I sometimes pack clothing on hangers with plastic dry-cleaning bags using the Z-fold method.

If you are going to be in a different place every day, would you still use the Bundle Method?

Yes! Of course, it is a bit different from being able to reach in and pull out one folded garment. The trade-off is you will have less creasing and spend less time ironing. Don't forget—with your efficient travel wardrobe, you will be working with only five to seven packed garments. You will get really good at quickly folding and unfolding the bundle.

Here are a few tips if you cannot unpack completely:

- Pack separates. They are easier to pack and unpack. To remove an inner item, you need only unfurl one or two items, reach your hand in, and slip out what is needed.

- When you arrive at your hotel, open your suitcase and unfurl the bundle. Let the sleeves and bottoms hang out of the sides of the bag. This will make each item accessible to you and give garments a chance to breathe and rest. Hang up your core pouch. In the morning, simply refold the bundle.

- Learn to think ahead about what you will need. Keep what you will want access to out of the bundle and either lay it on top or tuck it into the corners of your bag.

What is the difference between steamers and irons?

Steamers remove wrinkles from light- and medium-weight, absorbent fabrics, such as wool, silk, and synthetic blends. They do not work well on heavier weights of cotton. If you want a pressed, crisp look, an iron will be necessary.

How do you tie on the Flexo-line?

If your room has a shower, you can loop-knot the clothesline around the curtain rod and stretch it across to the shower head, looping it over. The line can also be doubled back on itself, if necessary.

P.S. Dental floss makes a handy clothesline.

Is there a product for a travel laundry kit that will take care of mildew?

The best way to take care of mildew is to wash in the hottest water that's safe for the fabric. If the stain remains, soak the garment in warm water with nonchlorine bleach and wash it again. The sun is also a natural bleach: treat fresh mildew with lemon juice and salt, and dry the garment in direct sunlight. Rinse and rewash the garment. Old mildew stains are almost impossible to remove.

How do you carry medicines?

Get your prescription medicine in two separately labeled small bottles. Keep half your supply in your day bag and half in your main bag so that if you lose one bag you will still have your medicine. If you need to refrigerate medicine, carry a lightweight insulated bag with an icepack. Refreeze the pack each night at your hotel.

How do you prevent bottles of shampoo and other liquids from leaking when carried on airplanes?

To prevent leaks, fill your bottles two-thirds full, squeeze out the air, and close them. You can tape the caps and pack them in plastic zip-locking bags for additional protection.

How do you keep lipstick from melting in hot weather?

Try using lip pencil instead of lipstick or travel-packaged sample-sized lip glosses.

Isn't a security wallet hot to wear?

Unfortunately, there is no way around it—in hot weather, anything against your body can feel uncomfortable. The best security wallet to wear in hot weather is one where the strap is worn around your waist and the wallet hangs vertically on your hip like a pocket, tucked inside your slacks or skirt where it is easily accessible. Both the World Class Passport Carrier and the Eagle Creek Undercover Security Wallet can adjust to be worn like this. If you prefer a standard rectangular waist pouch, choose one with a comfortable Coolmax absorbent backing, such as the UnderCover Deluxe Security Belt by Eagle Creek. All wallets should be treated inside to protect contents from moisture.

Are security wallets waterproof?

All security wallets are water-repellent so that they will resist perspiration moisture. In very warm weather, however, the contents can become damp. You can provide extra protection by encasing the contents in a zip-locking bag or the waterproof, resealable cover made by Omniseal. If you want to swim with your valuables, use a Seal Pack or other watertight wallet specifically designed to be submersible in water.

How much does a typical carry-on bag weigh when full?

My one bag with two wardrobes and all accessories weighs 25 pounds. This is about the most you would want to pack. If you take two bags, you can divide this weight, which will make the luggage easier to carry.

Does a 45-inch carry-on bag really fit under the seat?
The 45-inch bags (up to 22 inches long) do go under the seat in most planes. Rigid-frame bags, however, are more difficult to maneuver into place. Commuter or trans-Pacific flights, smaller aircraft, and aisle seats will be exceptions and may accommodate only 20-inch bags. Check the carry-on regulations for your airlines before you buy your luggage.

Aren't luggage carts a hassle?
This depends entirely on your situation. The lack of a luggage cart is a hassle if you have more than one bag. Carts are also versatile. They offer wider wheels and step sliders for added stability, and you can use them with any bag you already own. They do require that you stop and unload and collapse them before boarding the plane, and they must be stored separately. If you need only one carry-on and are planning to buy a bag, then wheeled luggage, such as the Rollaboard by Travelpro, will eliminate the need for an extra piece.

Does the steel cable in the World Class Passport Carrier set off the metal detector at the airport?
No, I've never heard of that happening.

Can I carry on my Swiss Army knife?
In short, no. You may only take a plastic or blunt butter knife with a blade under 4 inches on the plane. Scissors must be blunt and under 4 inches also. Anything larger must be packed in checked baggage. Swiss Army knives and the like will be confiscated at security. Sometimes there is a kiosk at the checkpoint where you can mail prohibited items home. An alternative is to buy at your destination or ship items ahead.

What do you do if U.S. Customs wants to inspect your belongings?

Let them! To decrease the time it takes to repack in case customs asks you to undo your bundle, use the Quick-Fix Method before coming home: Lay all your garments in the bag, stacking the collars in one direction. Drape the sleeves out. Drape the bottoms out. Put in your core pouch. To close the bundle, bring all the left sleeves in, then all the right sleeves. Then bring in the bottom. Voilà! There is your bundle. It is easy to unfurl and to close up again if you get stopped at customs. Remember, don't tempt customs. Have all your paperwork and declarable items ready and waiting to be inspected.

THE LAST-MINUTE PACKER'S QUICKLISTS

There's no way around it—packing less means planning more, at least the first few times you travel this way. Start this process as soon as you confirm your travel plans.

Planning in a Nutshell

Resolve that you want to travel light. This may be the hardest thing to do, but it has a major payoff in the end. Trust me—it's true.

Start a preliminary packing list. The following information will direct it:

1. Find out about the weather, local customs, and conditions—note clothing and gear needed. Think about what types of fabrics will provide the functions you need and which layering pieces you may need. Consider style as well.

2. Write down your planned activities and events; note clothing and gear needed.

3. Take note of things you absolutely can't do without to make you a happy traveler, even if they seem frivolous—you'll make up for the added load by cutting back somewhere else.

4. Peruse the checklists in this book. See if they remind you of something you need or haven't thought of. Make notes on your list.

5. Call your hotel(s) to confirm amenities, such as hairdryers. Discuss with your travel companion who will carry what (don't duplicate). Eliminate from your list gear you don't need.

6. Decide how you will do your laundry on the road. Hand wash? Dry clean? Determine appropriate fabrics you'll need.

7. Review your wardrobe for suitable clothing, accessories, and shoes. Make up outfits and note items needed to complete them. Choose a coordinating color scheme and stick to it.

8. Refine your packing list. Cut down wherever possible. Be ruthless!

9. Shop at stores, through catalogs, and online. Give yourself as much time as possible. Shop in fall and winter for warm-weather basics, such as thinly knit wool sweaters and tops.

10. Assemble your medical, toiletry, and other kits. Little items take forever to assemble and are easily forgotten at the last minute (see chapter 3). Always keep them at the ready for carefree packing.

11. Practice packing. See what fits and what can be eliminated. Try to carry it a distance. If it's too heavy, eliminate more. (If you're having trouble here, go back to #1!)

12. After your trip, review your list. Cross out items you didn't need and write down things you wished you had packed. Store this list in your suitcase or security wallet or on your computer. Next time, you'll use this information to cut down even more.

Last-Minute Packer's To-Do List

Here's what needs to be done in the few days before you leave:

- Check the current weather at destination(s).
- Make and finalize your packing list; do last-minute shopping.

- Wash and iron clothes; fasten all zippers and buttons.
- Pick up dry cleaning.
- Pick up traveler's checks.
- Get foreign cash—at least $50 in each denomination.
- Get $1 bills for tips.
- Establish PIN numbers for your credit and ATM cards.

TIP: I like to start packing my security wallet a couple of days ahead, as this needs to be RIGHT! All the other stuff in unimportant compared to your needed documents.

Pack your valuable documents, tickets, and money in your security wallet. (Don't forget photo ID and/or passport—you can't even get on the plane without these!!)

Packing Time

- Get out your packing list—make one if you haven't already!
- Assemble your documents, money, and ID in security wallet.
- Assemble all your travel clothing, including underwear, socks, shoes, and accessories.
- Get out your suitcase or garment bag and day bag.
- Gather your packing aids: organizer pouches or zip-locking bags, core pouch, shoe covers, plastic dry-cleaning bags, hangers, plastic bag for wet or soiled items, and so on.
- Make up your medical, toiletry, and other kits.
- Charge your computer, cell phone, and whatever else needs it.
- Pack your business case, tote bag, or daypack. This can be heavy and go under the seat.
- Pack your suitcase. Keep it as light as possible so you can lift it overhead.

Preparation for Leaving Home Quicklist

- Choose a home contact who will able to send you anything you need in an emergency. Make a contact book for your home contact with copies of all your documents, itineraries, phone numbers, information, emergency information, and so on (see pp. 50–51).

- If you are leaving your children at home, make a binder of information for caregivers—such as local emergency numbers; medical, dental, and allergy information; medical authorization; friends' and schools' phone numbers; maps; children's schedule; and directions. Arrange for rides to and from activities, if needed. Notify friends that you will be away. Review the children's plan and your itinerary with your children before you leave.

- Engrave your valuables. If something is stolen, it has a better chance of being retrieved.

- Consider taking valuables to a safe-deposit box.

- Pay your bills before you leave, or arrange for someone else to do so.

- Stop the newspaper.

- Stop the mail and all deliveries, or ask a neighbor to collect all deliveries.

- *Don't* change the phone message on your answering machine.

- Arrange with neighbors for the garbage cans to be put out on the curb and replaced after pickup.

- Arrange for a gardener to keep up the yard.

- Make it look like you're home—leave curtains and blinds in normal position, park your car in the driveway, or ask a neighbor to park there periodically.

- Plug in timers to turn on lights and a radio or television.
- Make sure the heat is turned down or off and all burners are off.
- Lock all doors and windows.

The following lists come in handy when you're packing in a hurry.

The Bare Essentials Checklist

☐ security wallet (contents pp. 48–49)

☐ photo ID/passport

☐ important documents (contents pp. 50–51)

☐ techno-gear as desired, with chargers/batteries/cables

☐ travel alarm clock or watch with alarm

☐ toiletry kit

☐ medical/first-aid kit

☐ clothing care kit

☐ travel umbrella, packable raincoat

☐ hat, sunscreen, insect repellent

☐ water bottle (with purifier, if needed), snack food

☐ flashlight or reading light, batteries

☐ notebook and pen

☐ book, portable tape or CD player

☐ small camera, film/media, batteries

☐ set of ear plugs

☐ plastic bag for wet or soiled items

☐ fold-up, expandable nylon tote bag

☐ photographs of your family

Organizing Yourself

The Basic Bags

- [ ] your main bag (21- or 22-inch carry-on, 24-inch checkable bag, or garment bag)
- [ ] your day bag (daypack, duffel, tote)
- [ ] last-minute bag (can be your day bag)
- [ ] security wallet
- [ ] day wallet or nylon pouch
- [ ] core pouch(es)—one for each bundle
- [ ] bags for kits—plastic resealable bags, nylon organizer bags, stuff sacks
- [ ] shoe covers

Main Suitcase Checklist

Try to keep this bag light enough to lift overhead. Pack heavy items in your day bag so you can stow them under the seat.

- [ ] luggage ID, inside and out
- [ ] luggage lock
- [ ] envelopes with confirmations, itinerary, trip notes
- [ ] clothing
- [ ] shoes
- [ ] lingerie
- [ ] handbag
- [ ] non in-flight gear, including the following:
  - travel clock
  - clothing care kit

- picnic kit
- water purifier
- extra batteries
- small appliances, cell-phone charger
- half of prescription medicine
- small gifts

☐ In outside pockets, if any

- stowable raincoat
- hat
- toiletry kit
- fold-up, expandable nylon tote
- small umbrella

Tote Bag Checklist

Outside Pockets

☐ luggage lock

☐ luggage ID, inside and out

☐ boarding passes, customs documents, receipts, local currency

☐ any other documents that need to be accessible for boarding and leaving the plane or train

☐ addresses

☐ pen and notebook, or office supply kit

☐ emergency items: knife, flashlight, compass, tool kit

☐ bandanna, handkerchief

☐ prescription medicines, cup

☐ first-aid kit

Middle of Bag

☐ in-flight toiletry kits: moist towelettes, toilet-seat covers, sanitary items, toothbrush and toothpaste, mints or mouthwash, comb, lip balm, moisturizer, headache reliever, antacid, antihistamine, and so on

☐ eye-care supplies

☐ cosmetics/pocket mirror

☐ water bottle, snack

☐ family photos (in plastic cover)

☐ wallet (for minimal cash, receipts only)

☐ coin purse

☐ eyeglasses, sunglasses

☐ in-flight reading material, work

☐ computer and computer equipment

☐ cell phone, pager

☐ walkman, tapes

☐ in-flight accessories:

- travel pillow
- eyeshades
- earplugs
- jet-lag remedy, melatonin, Dramamine, and so on
- thick socks or slippers
- flashlight
- phrasebook, guidebook
- map, magnifier, highlighter pen

Bottom of Bag

- [ ] jewelry
- [ ] sweater or jacket
- [ ] extra shirt and underwear, swimsuit (if checking other luggage)
- [ ] umbrella
- [ ] keys
- [ ] camera and film
- [ ] half of your traveler's checks
- [ ] important documents, vouchers, receipts (see pp. 50–51)
- [ ] small appliances

Security Wallet Checklist

- [ ] photo ID
- [ ] passport
- [ ] credit cards
- [ ] ATM card
- [ ] cash, U.S. and local currency
- [ ] traveler's checks
- [ ] checks
- [ ] long-distance calling card
- [ ] tickets
- [ ] driver's license
- [ ] auto club card
- [ ] copies of medical and eyeglass prescriptions
- [ ] 3 x 5-inch card with emergency phone numbers and medical allergies
- [ ] student ID card

- [ ] train pass or voucher
- [ ] address list
- [ ] visa(s)
- [ ] extra passport photos
- [ ] other documents (see pp. 50–51)

Toiletry Kit (Small Sizes Only)

These items are often forgotten on the day of travel, so make a duplicate kit that is ready to go at all times.

Hotel-with-Amenities Trip

- [ ] eye-care supplies
- [ ] facial cleanser
- [ ] toothbrush, holder or cap
- [ ] toothpaste
- [ ] dental floss
- [ ] antiperspirant
- [ ] razor and blades or shaver
- [ ] shaving cream
- [ ] nail clipper
- [ ] travel soap
- [ ] comb/folding brush
- [ ] pocket mirror

Self-Sufficient Trip

- [ ] shampoo
- [ ] conditioner
- [ ] moisturizer
- [ ] hairdryer (dual-voltage with adapter plugs for foreign travel)

Makeup/Beauty

- [ ] foundation
- [ ] eye shadow
- [ ] blush
- [ ] lip pencil
- [ ] lipstick
- [ ] mascara
- [ ] eye pencil
- [ ] other

Health/First-Aid Kit

- [ ] sufficient supply of all prescription medications
- [ ] antidiarrhea medication (e.g., Pepto-Bismol tablets)
- [ ] acetaminophen or ibuprofen
- [ ] antacid (e.g., Alka-Seltzer tablets)
- [ ] antiseptic pads
- [ ] antibiotic ointment (for cuts and scratches), cotton swabs
- [ ] anti-itch balm or 1% hydrocortisone cream (for insect bites)
- [ ] adhesive tape, gauze bandages, first-aid strips, and so on
- [ ] motion-sickness remedy
- [ ] sunscreen
- [ ] lip balm
- [ ] decongestant or antihistamine
- [ ] insect repellent
- [ ] thermometer (nonmercury)
- [ ] travel dental kit
- [ ] water-purification tablets or equipment, if needed

Clothing-Care Kit

- [ ] sewing kit
- [ ] multipurpose travel soap
- [ ] stain treatment
- [ ] clothesline/clips
- [ ] inflatable hanger
- [ ] sink stopper
- [ ] shoe shine pads, if needed
- [ ] plastic bag for wet or soiled clothing
- [ ] Packtowl
- [ ] lint brush or roller
- [ ] steamer, iron, or wrinkle-remover spray

Emergency Kit

For that "just in case" level of protection, carry the following in a small, plastic, resealable bag or a small nylon pouch. Tuck it in your purse, pocket, briefcase, or inside your underwear! You can find individually wrapped first-aid and nonprescription drugs in pharmacies and well-stocked travel stores.

- [ ] antiseptic pad
- [ ] antibiotic ointment
- [ ] adhesive bandages, gauze bandage
- [ ] moist towelettes
- [ ] ibuprofen
- [ ] Pepto-Bismol tablets
- [ ] tiny sewing kit with needle and thread, buttons, safety pins
- [ ] a few tissues

☐ folded-up toilet seat cover

☐ personal hygiene pad, tampon

☐ condom

Picnic Kit

☐ spoon

☐ pocket knife (remember security restrictions)

☐ hot/cold cup

☐ cutting board

☐ dual-voltage beverage heater (with adapter plugs)

☐ Packtowl wipe-up cloth

☐ small plastic plate (optional)

☐ bottle stopper

Emergency Card

In your security wallet, carry a 3 x 5-inch card with the following information. (Also put a copy of the card, *minus your credit card number and Social Security number*, in your companion's luggage and in each piece of your own luggage.)

☐ home-contact phone number

☐ credit card number

☐ phone number to report lost credit card

☐ travel agent

☐ doctor

☐ lawyer

☐ Social Security number

☐ codes (if any)

- [ ] passport number
- [ ] driver's license number

For Office Supplies see pp. 76–77.

For Computer Equipment see p. 78.

For Women's Packing List see p. 121.

For Men's Packing List see p. 122.

For Business Travel see pp. 154–163.

Dear Overpackers:

I hope that *The Packing Book* has been helpful to you. If you have any

- Travel tips
- Overpacked luggage "horror" stories
- Positive carry-on experiences
- Favorite luggage or gear
- Clothing ideas and experiences
- Packing tips

or simply any feedback or suggestions at all, please write to me:

> Judy Gilford
> c/o Ten Speed Press
> P.O. Box 7123
> Berkeley, CA 94707

Your tips may be included in my next book!

Index

Laptops (*continued*)
　converters and transformers for,
　　84–85, 152
　operation of, during flight, 10, 153
　resources for, 231
　weight of, 152
　wireless access for, 152
"Last-minute" bags, 14, 27
Laundry, 68, 70, 108–11, 199, 218
Layering
　for adults, 100–108
　for children, 199–200
Leg pouches, 48
Light bulbs, 85
Lipstick, 244
Locks, 38
Lonely Planet's Travel Vault, 51
Loungewear, 96–97
Luggage. *See also* Carry-ons; Checked
　　luggage
　for business travel, 151–52
　buying guidelines for, 31–36
　children and, 188–90
　color of, 32
　coordinating, 16
　damaged, 31–32, 39–40, 224
　fabric for, 32–33
　floors of, 35
　handles on, 33
　identifiers for, 37
　labeling, 37–38, 39
　locks for, 38
　lost, 1
　resources for, 226–30
　security and, 214–15
　special features on, 35–36
　straps for, 34, 38
　tags for, 37–38
　types of, 15–31
　warranties on, 31–32
　weatherproofing, 33
　wheeled, 18, 21–25, 34
　zippers on, 35
Luggage carts, 36–37, 245

M

Mace, 9
Makeup, 63, 257
Maps, 71
Martial-arts equipment, 9
Matches, 10
Medications
　carrying, 243
　checklist for, 55
　security and, 9, 215
Memory sticks, 51
Men
　adventure wardrobe for, 180–81
　basic wardrobe for, 122
　business travel wardrobes for,
　　160–62
　leisure travel wardrobes for, 168–71,
　　173–74, 176–77
　wardrobe color planner for, 92
Metal detectors, 30
Micro Filter Bottle (Katadyn), 59
Mildew, 243
Money
　accessible, 49
　exchange calculators, 75
　security wallets for, 45–48
Money belts, 48
Mosquito netting, 57
Motion-sickness remedy, 60
Mountain travel, 182

N

Nail clippers, 9
Nail files, 9
Neck pouches, 47
Nightlights, 203
No-Jet-Lag, 59

O

Office-on-Wheels (Tutto), 29, 229
Office supplies, 76–77
Outlet types, 78–80
Overhead compartments
　courtesy and, 12

Notes